To Renée Behnke—

Viva Les Vegan Chefs—

and the joys of Ser La Table!

Anne Kupper Pinella

Personal Favorites

Personal Favorites

The Chefs of *Las Vegas*

Heidi Knapp Rinella

Stephens Press, LLC

A *Las Vegas Review-Journal* Book

Editor: Joan Tammariello
Photographer: Jeff Scheid
Creative Directors: Chris Wheeler and Sue Campbell
Design and Production: Evan Field and Dan Love

ISBN: 1-932-173-13-7

CIP Data Available

Stephens
Press LLC

A Stephens Media Group Company
P.O. Box 1600, Las Vegas, Nevada 89125-1600

www.stephenspress.com

Printed in Hong Kong

Dedication

To Frank, Aynsley and Aubrey

Contents

Acknowledgements

This book wouldn't exist without the lifelong interest in and dedication to food instilled in me by my parents, Jean and the late Eugene Knapp, who also fostered my adventurous spirit with their thirst for travel and willingness to try offbeat foods well before it was fashionable.

I also owe a limitless debt of gratitude to my husband, Frank, the only man I've ever known brave enough to eat lion. ("What did it taste like?" I asked. "About how you'd expect cat to taste," he replied.) Frank and, later, our daughters, Aynsley and Aubrey, have been by my side as I ventured into restaurants near and far, and have been my critical companions as I reviewed spots in Las Vegas and Southwest Florida during more than two decades. They've also been my own best critics as I experimented — sometimes successfully, sometimes not — with unfamiliar dishes at home.

Thanks, also, to Sherman Frederick, Thomas Mitchell and Frank Fertado, who expressed their faith when they selected me as the Las Vegas *Review-Journal's* restaurant critic and have been continuously supportive. And I must mention Ron Thornburg of the Ogden (Utah) *Standard-Examiner*, and Keith Moyer, publisher of the Minneapolis *Star Tribune*, who launched my critiquing career all those years ago. Also Joan Tammariello, who exhibited a truly impressive amount of patience as she edited this book, Jeff Scheid, who photographed it, and of course my publisher, Carolyn Hayes Uber, whose friendship and support I treasure.

And finally, I would like to express my appreciation to all of the chefs and their colleagues who contributed to this book, and to the chefs, cooks, sommeliers and other foodies who have shared their knowledge and friendship along the way. Your dedication and enthusiasm are always inspiring.

Foreword

Known for a half-century for its overflowing bargain buffets and plentiful prime-rib specials, Las Vegas' culinary picture began to shift focus during the early '90s.

Back in the "old days," the name of the game when it came to Las Vegas dining — er, eating — was to supply a surfeit of food that was cheap and available 24/7. The quality of the cuisine was not that important as long as it was filling. No one knew the names of the cooks. They didn't even call them chefs in those days.

Casino executives had long held to the theory that restaurants were merely an adjunct to the casinos — a loss-leader method of pulling the tourists in off the streets and keeping 'em fueled for more time at the tables or slots. Local legend holds, in fact, that the first Las Vegas buffet was a low-cost late-night spread designed to keep audience members from exiting after the last show of the evening.

That approach started to evolve in the early '90s, as volcanoes began to erupt on the Strip, pyramids and castles followed and Las Vegas decided to reinvent itself as a Boomer-friendly family destination. Suddenly, non-gaming activities such as high-end shopping and fine dining became a new niche; it's no coincidence that the city's first celebrity-chef restaurant, Wolfgang Puck's Spago, helped launch its first "shoppertainment" destination, The Forum Shops at Caesars.

Puck's pioneering caravan across the desert would be followed by a long line of culinary immigrants that continues to the present and has made Las Vegas one of the most exciting dining destinations in America, maybe even the world.

Today, tourism and casino officials have embraced the importance of fine dining in drawing visitors to Las Vegas. In 2004, the Global Gaming Expo for the first time featured a food-and-dining component, in recognition of the fact that this segment of the industry accounted for 57 percent of total revenue in 2003, compared to 43 percent 10 years before, and is growing faster than gaming revenue.

Those restaurants, however, could not exist without the men and women who work long and hard in them and whose creative spirit and dedication to their craft is sown for 35 million visitors a year to reap. A complete list would be exhaustive, but includes Emeril Lagasse, the Maccioni family, Charlie Palmer, Jean-Georges Vongerichten, Thomas Keller, Mary Sue Milliken and Susan Feniger, Piero Selvaggio and Luciano Pellegrini, Joachim Splichal and, among the most recent arrivals, Hubert Keller, Bobby Flay, Rick Moonen and Alain Ducasse.

They also include the people profiled in this book — people like Jay Hamada, a Japanese immigrant who fell in love with

Las Vegas on his first visit during the late '50s and eventually launched a local chain of restaurants, and Andre Rochat, a French expatriate who forged a path through the fine-dining wasteland in 1980. They also include Todd English, Michael Mina, Tom Colicchio, Cindy Hutson and Puck, who found fame with restaurants in numerous cities; Marc Poidevin, David Robins, Alex Stratta and Julian Serrano, who made their names in other cities but now dedicate themselves solely to Las Vegas, and Michael and Wendy Jordan, who proved that fine food would be appreciated in the suburbs as well as on the Strip.

Heidi Knapp Rinella is a highly acclaimed professional food writer and, in my personal opinion, one of the best in the field, whether in Las Vegas, which she calls home, or nationally, of which she regularly has a purview. Her treatment of the chefs in this book provides not only insightful and inspiring profiles of each but also includes the ambiance and inspiration of each of their establishments. The addition of individual chefs' personal favorites makes this all the more fun to read and use.

— *Tim Zagat*

Co-Chairman, Zagat Guide LLC

Introduction

Oh, what that old rascal Beldon Katleman hath wrought. Katleman is generally regarded as the father of the Las Vegas buffet, which has become a city institution. He was the owner of the El Rancho Vegas Hotel back in the early '40s, and — in time-honored Las Vegas tradition — was looking for a way to keep gamblers at his tables.

Katleman came up with the idea for a midnight feast. Since Las Vegas still was pretty much the Wild West back then, he called it the Midnight Chuck Wagon Buffet. And a few trips around the chuck wagon cost visitors a single dollar.

It's never taken long for good ideas to spread in Las Vegas, and that was the case with Katleman's brainstorm. The budget buffet became a staple of a Las Vegas visit — we might lose money at the tables, the tourists figured, but by God, we'll eat well — and today nearly every casino of any size has its own. The Las Vegas Convention and Visitors Authority estimates that 80 percent of visitors to Las Vegas eat at buffets.

But while the buffet became the standard of Las Vegas dining, an epicurean revolution was slowly transforming the way Americans eat, and the movement would eventually extend to Las Vegas, with Wolfgang Puck as the pioneer. In 1992, Puck opened a Spago at The Forum Shops at Caesars. It wasn't an instant hit — visiting National Finals Rodeo fans lined up at Puck's open kitchen, thinking it was a buffet — but residents and visitors alike quickly saw that there was something more there, and that they wanted to share in it.

Once Puck broke the ice, he was followed by a veritable parade of celebrity chefs. A few tested the waters, failed, and turned tail, but most found success and stayed on, some of them in time opening additional Las Vegas restaurants.

Today, the city is considered one of the leading restaurant cities in the world — a destination for people interested in fine dining. And as this book goes to print, Las Vegas is poised for another wave of restaurants run by big-name celebrity chefs, some of them even more famed than those who have come before.

Personal Favorites is a celebration of Las Vegas' gustatorial greatness. Twelve of the most prominent figures in the city's restaurant world agreed to participate — to tell their stories and share a few recipes for their own personal favorites.

Andre Rochat

Andre's French Restaurant

"So many classic dishes have been forgotten because so many young chefs don't know anything about cooking. Not that it's all bad; I'm not saying that. But all of this trendy cooking comes and goes. The traditional cooking, it'll never die."

It's a perfect, neat circle: Andre Rochat remembers standing on a stool to operate a sausage stuffer in his parents' butcher shop in France, using the device's horn to force a carefully balanced mixture of meat and seasonings into yards of transparent natural casings.

Rochat still stuffs sausages today, but these are more likely to be a lot less traditional than those of his childhood — maybe filled with lobster and served with spicy crawfish sauce. They're destined for one of Rochat's own restaurants, Andre's French Restaurant, Andre's at the Monte Carlo, Alizé, or Mistral. And

they're the product of Rochat's peripatetic experiences between then and now.

Today, Rochat has a place in the pantheon of Las Vegas' most celebrated chefs, but his near-Dickensian early years were unlike those experienced by most of his colleagues. A native of La Rochette, a pastoral little village in the French Alps, Rochat was born near the end of World War II in a country that was still staggering under the weight of two catastrophic wars.

"There was nothing — nothing at all," he said. "The economy was down to zero. The country was just beginning to rebuild. I remember waiting in line to buy a pound of

sugar. At the time, we used to wear wooden shoes." Light came from oil lamps. Radio was a luxury until Rochat was 5 or 6 years old.

The times were bleak, but the shop kept the family going — and it was a true family affair. "Since 5 years old, I worked in the store, period," he said. "Life was school and store. After school, you had a piece of bread and chocolate" and then it was back to work in the store.

Rochat is known today for his exacting standards and willingness to work long, hard hours to maintain them. And it seems that pattern isn't new. "I had an independent attitude all along," he said with a wry smile. That attitude showed itself in such episodes as the time he ran away with some traveling gypsies — at age 5. ("My father caught me in the next village.")

His father apparently decided that the boy's independent streak could stand just a little taming, and sent him off at age 7 to a Catholic boarding school. The schedule is clearly is burned into his memory: Up at 6 a.m., study from 7 to 8:30, breakfast at 8:30, class from 9 a.m. to noon, lunch at noon, recess from 1 to 2 p.m., study from 2 to 3 p.m., class from 3 to 5 p.m., recess with bread, chocolate, and milk from 5 to 5:30, then dinner, more studying and finally off to bed at 9:30. Rochat endured six days a week of this for seven years, with infrequent visits home.

And then he was 14 and school was out. "I decided," Rochat said, "to become a chef." While the rest may be history, the road ahead would not be a smooth one; whatever discipline Rochat may have picked up in school would be needed in the years to come.

First, he returned to the business of butchering, sometimes processing 70 to 100 rabbits at a stretch. Experience

Andre Rochat's first Las Vegas establishment, Andre's French Restaurant, is still the most charming, in the opinion of his most loyal fans. Located in a former residential neighborhood in downtown Las Vegas — which makes Rochat a downtown redevelopment visionary, whether by design or not — it's filled with Country French charm and cozy rooms; you'll feel you're in a home, which is exactly how this building started out. The menu changes with the season but might include such dishes as golden osetra caviar with buckwheat blini, oven-roasted rack of lamb with violet mustard sauce, or roasted saddle of rabbit stuffed with braised rabbit leg, shallots, and tarragon. Dinner only. Rochat has three other restaurants in Las Vegas — the elegant jewel box Andre's at the Monte Carlo, Mistral at the Las Vegas Hilton and the sleek and stunning Alizé, whose glass walls afford an impressive fiftieth-story view of the dazzling necklace that the Strip represents as it laces through the valley of gemlike lights, dinner only. Andre's French Restaurant, 401 S. Sixth St.; 702-385-5016 or www.andresfrenchrest.com.

showed; he could clean a rabbit in less than two minutes. Then his father found him a position as an apprentice in Lyons, at the Michelin two-star Lyon de Lyons. The chef/owner was Paul Lacombe. "He was just as hard as my father," Rochat remembered.

That was clear from the beginning. Rochat had dressed up for his initial appearance at Lyon de Lyons, but as soon as his parents had departed and the apprenticeship officially began, Lacombe "made me clean the floors of the restaurant — all dressed up. That was my first night."

As an apprentice, he was given a room on the sixth or seventh floor of an ancient building, right under the eaves. There was one light bulb, no heat, no water. The walls were "insulated" with newspaper. His water frequently was frozen in its bottle.

The workday began at 8:30 a.m., ran until 2:30 p.m. and resumed at 5, not ending until about 11. He was allowed only water to drink. "Food for the employees was the gizzards and the necks of the chickens, and leftovers," Rochat said. "The old man was rough." And as an apprentice, Rochat didn't get paid for the first six months. "After that, I started to make $1 a month," he said.

Apprentices are grunts, and required to do the grunt work. Rochat and a cohort cleaned all of the fish, vegetables and wild game; he remembers cleaning and plucking tiny birds, and wild hares that were smelly and full of shot. On Saturdays,

Rochat and the other apprentice would take apart and clean the entire kitchen, even polishing the stove with sandpaper.

After the second year, Rochat starting rising at 5 a.m. to go to market with Lacombe. "He and (eminent chef) Paul Bocuse were drinking champagne," he remembered. "I'd carry all the cases to the car. Sometimes they'd be so loaded. . . ." But Lacombe had a devotion to quality that would become a habit for Rochat and serve him well in the years to come. "Everything was fresh every day," he said.

And so he maintained, and he learned, and he saved his meager earnings to buy a battered Renault. When he made one of his infrequent trips home, he left the car at the edge of the village rather than explain the purchase to his demanding father, "because he would never let me have it," he said. "He never knew."

After three years as an apprentice, Rochat stood for his professional certificate. At 17, he went to work in a friend's restaurant in a beautiful old monastery outside Lyon. But his feet itched. "I wanted to travel," Rochat said. "La Rochette was way too small for me."

He was drafted into the Alpine Hunters — a "very tough" military unit that "was still too close to home." A doctor who had been a neighbor in La Rochette had some connections in the military. Rochat wanted to travel? He could do it in the navy.

He was assigned to the Marcel le Bian, a submarine that could go deeper than almost any other. They would be making an

expedition to Puerto Rico because of the deep waters there; the submarine could dive to 28,000 feet. Rochat would be not on the submarine, but on a flat-bottomed supply ship with an unconventional bottom-mounted propulsion system.

"We crossed the whole Atlantic at three knots," he remembered. "It took one and a half months. Of course we ran out of food." So they left the lights on and caught the fish that flopped onto the deck. For four months in Puerto Rico, Rochat was the ship's cook. The stove had a diesel burner. When the ship would roll, the stove would smoke or the flame would go out. And, Rochat said, "it stunk like hell."

After he finished his duty, Rochat went to work in a private club in Paris. Then an offer came from a restaurant — a beautiful place with terraces reaching down to the river. Here Rochat would once again have to summon his self-discipline: The restaurant had no kitchen. "I had an old charcoal stove right on the dirt in the basement," he said.

That didn't mean that less was expected of him. "I would do banquets, sometimes for 300 people, working 20 hours a day," he said. His days started with a 3 a.m. trip to the market, and he prepared lunch and dinner every day. "The stove would get so hot it would get red," he said. He had to take salt pills in the summer to ward off dehydration.

After five or six months, Rochat had his emigration papers. He arrived in Boston in 1965 with suitcase in hand and his chef's

knife wrapped in newspaper. While he was in Puerto Rico, he had met a woman who owned a Boston restaurant and she offered him a job. Now, he contacted the people who were managing it for her.

"They got me a little room, and I started to work," Rochat said. "At the time, I had about 3 bucks in my pocket." He worked lunch and dinner for a year — at the same time working in a bakery from 3 to 9 a.m.

Rochat soon moved on, to a corporation that employed him in Boston and then transferred him as an executive chef to Alexandria, Virginia. Then it was on to The Madison in Washington, D.C., then to a position as executive sous chef for United Airlines in New York.

"That's when the chef used to fly in first class and carve the Chateaubriand," Rochat said. It was his first experience with a union shop — and being told to work 8 to 5. "It didn't take me long to be bored with that," Rochat said.

He went to work in a New York restaurant, but the cook, a friend, had family in Carson City, Nevada, and invited Rochat to make the move. He left New York in the spring of 1970 and became executive chef at the Golden Nugget in Carson City.

"This is the first place I ever got fired in my life," he said. "I refused to serve some of the stuff (the food and beverage director) wanted me to serve, so he fired me." But Rochat wasn't unemployed for long. He found a job as chef of the gourmet room in

an Incline Village hotel. And then he met a dancer from Las Vegas. After a year, he quit and they moved to Las Vegas to get married. It was 1971, and Rochat became sous chef at the Sands. He stayed there until 1973.

But desert plants weren't exactly growing under his feet. Rochat was looking around — and noticing there weren't many good bakeries in Las Vegas. "I decided to open a bakery, even through I wasn't a baker by trade," he said.

The Savoy French Bakery opened on Maryland Parkway in 1973, selling wholesale as well as retail. Rochat didn't have much in the way of equipment. He'd work 1,200 to 1,500 pounds of flour a night — "all by hand." And he can remember working from 1 a.m. Friday to 5 p.m. Sunday. "But the bakery was extremely successful," he said. Starring Strip entertainers would come by for lunch. "We had some great times there."

Still, Rochat was itching to open his own restaurant. He sold the bakery in 1977 and bought a house in downtown Las Vegas with a friend, Andre Chaiysal. Rochat returned to the Sands as sous chef. He was working from 5 a.m. to 1 p.m. with contractors converting the house into a restaurant, and then at the Sands from 2 to 11 p.m.

Andre's French Restaurant opened at 401 South Sixth Street in June 1980. "The week before we opened, Andre called me from the hospital," Rochat said. He said he had cancer. "This is no time to joke," Rochat told him. But it wasn't a joke. "He just gave up on life," Rochat said. Chaiysal died about a year later, at age 47.

Rochat would suffer other setbacks. He and his wife divorced. Despite the restaurant's location in the middle of busy downtown Las Vegas, lunch wasn't profitable, so Rochat eliminated it. In those days of high-flying interest rates, his bank loan was at 18 percent interest. "I paid that loan a few times over," he said sardonically.

He was down to working only about 16 hours a day. And then, in 1981, he was approached by a representative of the second-largest flour mill in France. The man wanted Rochat to open a wholesale bakery. Within the first year, they opened a retail store. And Rochat was back to the old grind — at the bakery from 5 a.m. to 5 p.m., then at the restaurant until midnight. He did it for a year. "It was just too many problems," he said.

After Rochat parted ways with the bakery, he enlarged the restaurant. But operating a fine French restaurant in a city known for its bargain buffets was not without its frustrations. "When I opened this place in 1980," Rochat said, gazing around his downtown restaurant, "I had the largest wine list in town. People would come and have highballs with dinner."

Still, he persevered; "people were getting more and more into wine." They were getting more and more into Rochat's restaurant as well. He started a club called the Bec Fin Society, which held special dinners that focused on specific provinces

of France and the foods and wine of those provinces, and different countries, as well. He held wine dinners. And one-item dinners, in which the eight courses would each have one item in common. "That was very different, very challenging," Rochat said. "The crew would really get into it."

Somehow, he found some time to relax, which is how he met wife and partner Mary Jane Jarvis. Jarvis was at Lake Mead on a friend's boat for a St. Patrick's Day party in 1985. She heard about this French chef who hung around the dock.

"Then here comes Andre around the dock on his big boat," she said. "I don't know if it was love at first sight as much as it was fun at first sight." By 1986, they were running the restaurant together.

Ten years later, they were approached by a customer who asked if they were interested in operating a second restaurant. Andre's at the Monte Carlo opened in 1997.

There were still plenty of frustrations. Rochat's venture of a casual bistro downtown ran into a spaghetti-like tangle of bureaucratic obstacles. "I thought it would be a good thing to get into downtown redevelopment," he said of Froggy's. "They killed me before I started." The venture that was expected to cost $250,000 ended up costing him $500,000.

But better days were ahead. A few years later, Jarvis had an auspicious conversation with a local casino developer. "George Maloof's always been a good customer

here," she said. Maloof was building The Palms. They talked. "He was so cool," she said. "He called Andre the next morning."

Alizé, on the top floor of The Palms, opened in November 2002 with an award-winning menu and an incomparable view of the city. Mistral followed in 2004. And Rochat hasn't ruled out further expansion. "If the opportunity comes, sure," he said. "I have a lot of good ideas, a lot of things I would like to do. If someone wants to listen to me, yeah."

He also likes the challenge of being a mentor to young people. "I train them, make sure they have pride in their work, enjoy their work," he said. He's proud that he's trained a number of chefs who have moved on to high-profile jobs.

And Rochat's philosophy remains unchanged. "For me, this business is not for me to make money," he said. "I don't care. I like the challenge. Our industry is going through a lot of different things. To me, the old style of cooking is still the best — getting the foundation, fresh product, the sauces. Whatever is on the plate has to have a reason to be on the plate — it has to enhance your main ingredient.

"So many classic dishes have been forgotten because so many young chefs don't know anything about cooking. Not that it's all bad; I'm not saying that. But all of this trendy cooking comes and goes. The traditional cooking, it'll never die."

♣

Andre Rochat's

PERSONAL FAVORITES

Jumbo Sea Scallops Wrapped in a Macadamia Nut Crust

Duck Breast with Green Peppercorn Plum Sauce

André's Fresh Lemon Tart

Andre Rochat's

Jumbo Sea Scallops Wrapped in a Macadamia Nut Crust
Served with a Citrus Beurre Blanc

For scallops:
8 jumbo sea scallops
½ pound raw unsalted macadamia nuts
Salt
Pepper
1 cup flour
2 eggs, beaten lightly
4 tablespoons unsalted butter
¼ cup cooking oil
4 sprigs sweet basil

For beurre blanc:
1 shallot, finely chopped
Butter for sautéing
½ cup dry white wine
Juice of 1 lime
Juice of 1 orange
3 sticks unsalted butter, softened

For scallops: Rinse scallops quickly with cold water. Pat dry with a towel.

Grate macadamia nuts with a rotary cheese grater into a bowl. (Do not use a food processor, as it turns the nuts into paste.)

Salt and pepper the scallops. Pass quickly into the flour, removing any excess. Pass the scallops through the eggs, then into the grated nuts. Be sure the scallops are completely coated at each step. Refrigerate until ready to cook.

For beurre blanc: In a pan, sauté the shallot briefly in a little butter until it just begins to soften; add the white wine and the citrus juice and reduce to a syrup. Add the butter slowly with a whip or blender.

NOTE: Beurre blanc is served as a warm sauce; if it is too hot, it will break.) Add salt and pepper to taste. Keep warm.

Heat a frying pan over medium heat and add the 4 tablespoons butter and the ¼ cup oil. Place the scallops in the pan. Brown one side, then turn onto the other side and place pan into a preheated 400° F oven for approximately 6 minutes. The scallops should be golden brown and firm to the touch.

To serve: place 2 to 3 tablespoons beurre blanc on each plate; place 2 scallops in the center of the plate. Garnish with basil leaves.

Serves 4.

12

Andre Rochat's

Duck Breast with Green Peppercorn Plum Sauce

4 single breasts of duck, boned and partially skinned
2 tablespoons butter
2 tablespoons oil
4 large red plums, pitted and cut into wedges
(divided use), plus additional for garnish
1 ½ cups heavy cream
1 tablespoon green peppercorns
2 tablespoons green peppercorn juice
¼ cup red wine vinegar
6 tablespoons black currant syrup (divided use)
¼ cup brandy
Chopped parsley
Salt
Pepper

In a sauté pan over medium heat, cook the duck breasts in butter and oil to medium rare. Remove the duck from the pan and keep warm; discard half of the fat.

Add 2 plums to pan; cook slowly and discard remainder of fat. Add the cream and reduce to the consistency of a light sauce.

In another pan, combine peppercorns, peppercorn juice, red wine vinegar, and 4 tablespoons black currant syrup. Reduce until there is a sweet/sour balance to the taste. Add the cream sauce from previous step, passing through a fine sieve.

In a third pan, cook remaining 2 plums, brandy, and remaining 2 tablespoons currant syrup until liquid becomes syrup.

To serve: cover bottom of hot dinner plates with peppercorn-cream sauce. Slice duck breast thinly. Arrange duck slices in fan shape over sauce. Place plum wedge on top in the center. Pour plum-brandy sauce over and sprinkle with parsley.

Serves 4.

Andre Rochat's

Andre's Fresh Lemon Tart

For sugar dough pie shell:
2 cups flour
2/3 cup sugar
10 tablespoons butter, softened
1 egg yolk
1 tablespoon cream

For filling:
6 eggs
5 egg yolks
1 cup fresh lemon juice
Zest of 2 lemons
1 1/2 cups sugar
2 sticks butter
Lemon wedges
Powdered sugar

For sugar dough: Preheat oven to 375° F. Mix flour and sugar. Add soft butter, egg yolk, and cream. Mix until all ingredients are incorporated. Do not overwork the dough. Let the dough rest for about 20 minutes in a cool environment. Roll the dough and place in a pie shell, removing excess from rim. Puncture bottom of dough with a fork to prevent bubbling.

Bake 8 to 10 minutes or until golden brown. Remove from oven; cool.

For filling: Put eggs, yolks, lemon juice, lemon zest, and sugar in a stainless steel bowl. Place bowl over boiling water and blend with whip until thick paste-like consistency; do not mix too aggressively.

Remove from hot water and add butter; whip slowly. Pour filling in shell and smooth the top with a spatula. Let cool in refrigerator.

Before serving: garnish with lemon wedges, sprinkle with powdered sugar, and brown with kitchen torch.

Serves 6 to 8.

16

Tom Colicchio

Craftsteak

*"Flavor has everything to do with picking something
and getting it to the table as soon as possible."*

"For me, recipes have never been the point," Tom Colicchio writes in the preface to his book *Think Like a Chef.* And that could well be viewed as elucidation of his philosophy about cooking.

Colicchio is the chef/owner of Craftsteak at the MGM Grand, as well as Craft and Grammercy Tavern in New York City. He's also widely recognized as one of the leaders of the back-to-basics revolution — a credit Colicchio shuns. "I don't think I created anything," he said, a little indignantly. "I think it's more retro than anything. I wouldn't credit myself with creating anything new."

The "it" Colicchio is referring to is Craftsteak's straightforward approach to food as evidenced by its menu, from which customers are invited to put together their own meals. If, for example, you're in the mood for beef, you can order that beef grilled, maybe as a New York strip or grassfed strip, or roasted, as a hangar steak or tenderloin, or braised, as shortribs or cheeks. You can choose the side dishes you'd like to go with it, such as roasted chanterelles or potato soufflé or soft polenta or English pea ravioli or spaetzle. You can choose a vegetable — maybe roasted, as in Jerusalem artichokes or cippolini onions, or sautéed, as in asparagus or snow peas, or braised, as in salsify or fennel, or pureed, as in parsnips or celery root. "People appreciate the simplicity," Colicchio said.

When Colicchio developed the concept for Craft, he was already a successful New York chef/restaurateur, gaining acclaim for Grammercy Tavern; Colicchio won the James Beard Foundation Best Chef New York award in 2000 and Craft was named the Best New Restaurant in America in 2002.

While he was developing his vision of Grammercy Tavern, interpreting and presenting his own particular style and philosophy about food to a growing clientele, he kept thinking about the concept of "adding by subtracting."

"What would happen if I removed everything?" he recalled musing. It was a trend he'd seen growing, and one he himself had furthered, continually "subtracting over the years," he said. "I kind of pushed up the evolution of all those dishes" in the creation of Craft.

There was a pragmatic aspect to his plan as well. Craft was born in 2000 because a co-op near Grammercy Tavern wanted some advice on putting the space to the best use.

"I thought it was a good business opportunity," Colicchio said. "I thought it was time for me to do another restaurant."

One problem: "I couldn't do the same thing I was doing around the corner." So he thought about how he liked to eat, and decided to concentrate on one ingredient at a time. "It was a novel idea," he said. "I thought it would work. I thought that would be a neat thing to pull off." At Craft, customers would get to play chef, employing as much creativity as they wished as they put together their meals.

But there would be a few rough spots. The early days were characterized by a bit of confusion — and some misinformation. "It was never the case that you ordered the meat and

At Craftsteak, Tom Colicchio's deconstructed approach to food means that some-thing as simple as a plate of green beans takes on new aplomb and uncommon appeal, thanks to the integrity of the ingredients and the methods used to prepare them. Colicchio's approach makes Craftsteak particularly popular with fellow chefs, but you'll no doubt also be drawn to the high-styled yet warm woody interior with its dangling old-fashioned, large-filament bare light bulbs, a long line of huge glass jugs, and cozy booths, some of them separated by metal chain-link curtains. The menu features a wide variety of meats — some of them grilled, some roasted, some braised — plus roasted seafood, vegetables prepared roasted or sautéed or braised, and an impressive selection of mushrooms. Dinner only. The MGM-Grand also is home to Collicchio's casual 'wichcraft, which elevates the sandwich to Craft levels. MGM Grand, 3799 Las Vegas Blvd. South; 702-891-7318 or www.mgmgrand.com.

the way you wanted it cooked," Colicchio said — which might, for example, have led to someone ordering a grilled brisket, not exactly a good idea. "We always chose the cooking method." Still, he concedes today, "It was a little too complicated. After the first month, we got rid of the condiments and sauces" from the choices offered.

Some people never could get used to the idea. "There are people who love Craft, and there are people who hate it," Colicchio said. One New York customer comes in for dinner three to four times a week, he said, and Craft seems to be popular with Hollywood stars.

There doesn't seem to be that love-it-or-hate-it fractionalization at Colicchio's Las Vegas restaurant. When Craftsteak opened in 2002, the city was receptive, he said. "In Las Vegas, people never had an issue with the menu," Colicchio said. "Ninety percent of the people are comfortable with the service. It's fun to watch the first time."

But don't think that just because the concept is simple and straightforward, there's any question of relaxed standards. Enter Craftsteak on a late afternoon and you might see the service staff sitting at a few tables, painstakingly wiping glass after glass, holding each one up to the light to be sure each tiny water spot has been eradicated. "Things should be done right," Colicchio said, "especially at this level."

That of course extends to the food. Food is laid bare when such a pure concept is

employed, so it's imperative that it be of the utmost quality and as fresh as possible. Colicchio's menus are seasonal and dictated by what's available. "Flavor has everything to do with picking something and getting it to the table as soon as possible," he said. Craftsteak's fish, for example, is served less than 24 hours after it leaves the market.

Colicchio has cultivated, as it were, some local farmers in New York, and he has some of their products shipped in for the Las Vegas restaurant. But he's also pleased with some of the foods that are more readily available in the West. One afternoon when Colicchio was visiting Craftsteak, chef de cuisine Chris Albrecht showed him some fresh chickpeas that had just arrived — something Colicchio said he had never seen before. "It's fun to bring in these products," he said.

Colicchio said he remains based in New York because he thrives on the city's energy. That's not unusual with big-name Las Vegas chefs, but some handle the arrangement more successfully than others. Too tight a rein, and you may hamstring the chef de cuisine from being able to present his or her best. Too loose a rein — and employing the wrong person — can also spell disaster. Colicchio comes to Las Vegas once a month for about four days at a time, but he clearly believes in giving Albrecht his head. "It's his kitchen," Colicchio said. "The key to growing any business is you have to put your ego aside."

And for Colicchio, mentor seems to be a role that fits comfortably. He's working to

help Craft's chef de cuisine start his own restaurant, and cooperated with another employee to open 'wichcraft, an upscale sandwich shop next to Craftbar, Colicchio's New York cafe. "If this is something you have a passion for, I'll help you do it. I want to find someone who has an idea," he said. "I think it's a smart business decision. Why wouldn't I want to help them?"

Colicchio had help along the way as well, from people who no doubt knew that this young chef would make his mark on the American culinary scene. He was born in Elizabeth, New Jersey, in 1962, to a family that understood well the pleasures that food could bring. Both of his parents were good cooks, he said, and he liked to bake alongside his grandmother and catch fresh fish with his grandfather (and fishing remains a passion today). He learned to enjoy the process of putting together food, and "I found I was pretty good at it."

When Colicchio was 15, he started cooking at a swim-club snack bar, kicking up the repertoire. He moved on to a Burger King, and soon his father suggested he consider culinary school. During Colicchio's junior year of high school, the two drove to the Culinary Institute of America in Hyde Park, New York, to take a look. But in order to enroll at the CIA, he'd need to gain some restaurant experience — something beyond Burger King — so Colicchio went to work in Evelyn's Seafood Restaurant in Elizabeth. His dedication to his craft became evident at Evelyn's; in his book, Colicchio recalls falling

asleep, standing up, after cleaning more than 100 pounds of shrimp. He worked as a prep cook, baker, and line cook. He bought a copy of Jacque Pepin's *La Technique* and started experimenting. He also learned from his first mentor, a venerable Southerner named Slim.

Eventually, Colicchio moved on to the Chestnut Tavern, a small family-run Italian restaurant where he learned to cut meat — a skill that would come in handy in the future. Then he moved to The Old Mansion, on the grounds of a country club, with two recent CIA grads running the kitchen. He figured he'd learn a lot. He figured wrong. "I'd have to make the Hollandaise sauce, because they would break it all the time," he said.

Time to move on again. His next stop would be the Hilton in Secaucus, New Jersey. He was barely out of his teens. "After a week, they promoted me to night chef," he said. "I was 20 years old and had a staff of 23."

Still, he didn't stay long — less than a year. He saw an ad for a sous chef for a "New American" restaurant in Short Hills, New Jersey, called 40 Main Street. They filled the sous chef position before Colicchio applied, but hired him as a cook.

He knew immediately that in this kitchen, he would learn. The menu changed daily in response to the market — a revolutionary idea at the time. The kitchen was a veritable incubator for creativity, and the young chef responded. But he needed to grow further. The sous chef told him he had to try the

New York market. Colicchio was hired at the cutting-edge Quilted Giraffe. Within three months, he was promoted to sous chef. He was 24. "At that point," Colicchio said dryly, "I decided not to go to cooking school."

Then he got a call from the owner of 40 Main Street, who needed a chef to replace one who had left suddenly. He and a friend took positions as co-chefs. Another friend arranged a working sojourn for him in France. The period would be both instructional and inspiring, leaving lasting impressions about the importance of fresh, top-quality ingredients.

The next few years were inspiring as well. Colicchio worked with Alfred Portale at Gotham, and with legend-in-the-making Thomas Keller at Rakel. He went to Virginia Beach to open a restaurant with an old friend. Then on to Mondrian in New York. Another working foray in France, this time with Michel Bras, a Michelin two-star chef who was a devotee of wild ingredients. Back to Mondrian.

Colicchio was beginning to garner critical acclaim outside the circles of chefdom. *The New York Times* bestowed three stars eight months after he took over as executive chef. *Food & Wine* named him one of the 10 best new chefs of 1990.

Still, Mondrian was doomed to fail. The customers were coming, but the rent was too high and the prices too low, and the economy had taken a hit. With Mondrian closing, Colicchio approached Danny Meyer, owner of the Union Square Café, about a collaboration.

They would take a 10-day trip to Italy together. "If we could travel together, we could work together," Colicchio remembered with a laugh. They could and they would. And the result was Grammercy Tavern.

The first restaurant of his own would be a work in progress for a while. While it received, Colicchio said, "two stars out of the gate" and a third a year later, "it took time," he said. "It took a lot of hard work to turn it around. No matter how good you are, things take time to work themselves out. They take time to gel."

They persevered, and to good result: "Everything we wanted Grammercy Tavern to be, it is today," he said. "Great food, great products, without pretense at all." It opened in 1994.

Like many other chefs who have restaurants in Las Vegas, Colicchio is dedicated to building the local clientele. "If we take care of locals," he said, "the tourists will find us. I think we're doing a pretty good job of that. I think we're establishing ourselves as a presence in Las Vegas."

Colicchio said he doesn't see a huge difference between the New York and Las Vegas markets. For instance, summers bring more families in both, he said. But the Las Vegas market tends to be a little more casual, and "also more festive. They're here to have a good time." They're also in more of a hurry than his customers in New York. In the Big Apple, he said, it's not uncommon for parties arriving at Craft to stay two or three hours. "Here,

they're out in an hour, hour and a half," he said. "Here, this is a small part of the evening."

In addition to the partnerships with some of his staff members, Colicchio is open to interesting opportunities. "There's always stuff to do," he said. "The opportunities that chefs have now — they weren't out there 20 years ago." Still, he said, he's turned down a number of offers for deals that just didn't seem right. "I'm not into growing for the sense of growing," he said. "We'll grow when it makes sense."

♥

Tom Colicchio's

PERSONAL FAVORITES

Beet Salad with Beet Vinaigrette

Braised Short Ribs

Polenta

Tom Colicchio's

Beet Salad with Beet Vinaigrette

For salad:
24 baby beets (see note)
3 tablespoons grapeseed oil
Kosher salt
Freshly ground black pepper

For vinaigrette:
1 cup plus 2 tablespoons extra-virgin olive oil
(divided use)
1 large shallot, peeled and sliced
¼ cup red wine vinegar
¾ teaspoon Dijon mustard
½ cup peeled chopped roasted beets (from salad)
Kosher salt
Freshly ground black pepper
16 whole fresh tarragon leaves for garnish

For salad: Preheat oven to 325 ° F. Trim the green tops and stringy bottoms from the beets. Wash the beets well.

Combine the beets and oil in a large bowl. Season the beets with salt and pepper to taste and toss to coat.

Line a roasting pan with aluminum foil (this prevents the pan from becoming discolored). Add the beets, cover the pan with more foil and roast until the beets can be easily pierced with a knife, about 40 minutes. Allow the beets to cool

slightly, then carefully peel them. Coarsely chop about 4 of the beets for the vinaigrette. Set the rest aside to cool.

For vinaigrette: Heat 2 tablespoons of the olive oil in a skillet over medium heat. Add the shallot and cook until it is soft and translucent, about 15 minutes, then transfer to a blender. Add the vinegar, mustard, chopped beets, and salt and pepper. Puree, then with the blender running, gradually add the remaining oil in a steady stream. Adjust the seasoning, if necessary, with salt and pepper.

Arrange the beets on plates (they may be served whole or halved). Season them with salt, then lightly dress with vinaigrette. Garnish with tarragon leaves.

Serves 4 as an appetizer.

NOTE: If you're buying beets in the greenmarket, try to buy different types along with the classic red, like golden beets, chiogas, and candy stripes; the color contrast makes for an especially striking presentation.

Tom Colicchio's

Braised Short Ribs

2 tablespoons peanut oil
Kosher salt
Freshly ground black pepper
4 large, meaty beef short ribs (about 4 pounds),
cut in half
1 small onion, peeled and chopped
1 carrot, peeled and chopped
1 stalk celery, peeled and chopped
3 cloves garlic, unpeeled
5 sprigs fresh thyme
8 fresh hot cherry peppers (or canned, if fresh
are unavailable)
½ cup sherry vinegar
2 to 3 cups chicken stock
2 sprigs of fresh tarragon

Preheat oven to 350° F. Heat the oil in a large, deep, ovenproof skillet over medium-high heat until it shimmers. Salt and pepper the ribs to taste and cook them, in batches, until they are nicely browned on all sides, about 20 minutes.

Remove the ribs and add the onion, carrot, celery, garlic, 2 sprigs of thyme, and salt and pepper to the skillet. Cook, stirring occasionally, until the vegetables begin to soften, about 5 minutes, then add the peppers (if you are using canned peppers, add them with the vegetables). Continue cooking until the vegetables are tender and browned, 5 to 10 minutes more.

Return the ribs to the skillet. Add the vinegar and enough stock to come up the sides but not over the ribs. Bring the braising liquid to a simmer. Add the tarragon and remaining thyme, then transfer the skillet to the oven and cook at a very gentle simmer (just an occasional bubble) for 1 hour. Turn the ribs and continue cooking until the meat is tender and comes easily away from the bone, about 1 ½ hours more.

Transfer the ribs and vegetables to a plate. Bring the braising liquid to a simmer and skim off the fat. Reduce the liquid slightly (just so it has a little body) then return the ribs and vegetables to the skillet. Simmer just long enough to reheat the ribs, then serve.

Serves 4 as a main course.

(Recipe also appears in *Think Like a Chef*, by Tom Colicchio. New York: Clarkson Potter/Publishers, 2000.)

Tom Colicchio's

Polenta

6 cups chicken stock
2 cups polenta (see note)
Kosher salt
Freshly ground black pepper
6 tablespoons butter
2 tablespoons extra virgin olive oil
Fresh-picked thyme for garnish

Bring the stock to a boil over high heat in a large saucepot. Whisking constantly, gradually add the polenta. Whisk until the polenta comes to a simmer, then reduce the heat to medium-low. Season with salt and pepper and gently simmer, stirring frequently with a wooden spoon, until done, about 45 minutes. Stir in the butter and olive oil, adjust the seasoning with salt and pepper, and garnish with cracked pepper and thyme.

Serves 6 as a side dish.

NOTE: Craftsteak uses polenta from Anson Mills in South Carolina. Anson Mills makes a fresh-milled organic corn with a coarser grind than traditional dried polenta. It is available in many gourmet markets, where, because it isn't dried, it's refrigerated. It is also available by mail order through *www.ansonmills.com*.

Jay Hamada

Hamada of Japan

"I never think about tomorrow, just today. Maybe I'm a gambler."

For restaurant owner Jay Hamada, life would prove to be a really big shoe. Hamada is a native of Japan whose introduction to America came during an appearance on *The Ed Sullivan Show* (a "really big shoe," as Sullivan said) back in 1958. And in similar larger-than-life fashion, he would come to fall in love with the wide-open, Wild West feeling of the United States, which is epitomized no better than in the wide-open, Wild West city of Las Vegas.

Hamada was born in 1932 in Uwajima in southwestern Japan, the son of a Japanese naval officer. "After the war," he said, "there was no more navy." And so, as the eldest of six children, Hamada was expected to make his own way in the world. Luckily, a millionaire family friend by the name of Zenso Ito had taken an interest in the young man and would treat him almost as a son. "He thought I had business sense, and I had good manners," Hamada said.

Ito, who lived in Kobe and imported Austin automobiles, offered to teach Hamada his trade. "He said, 'Come to Kobe, I'll train you.'"

Hamada also was an athlete — a speed-swimming champion in the breaststroke. And he knew how to dance — especially impressive to Ito, who knew well the role that the social graces could play in business.

*J*ay Hamada's East Flamingo Road flagship restaurant is a feast for the eyes with its elegant Japanese styling, subdued Japanese artifacts (no kitsch here), and serene, peaceful atmosphere. It's also a uniquely accessible restaurant, with its various dining areas bringing even American novices the principal aspects of Japanese cuisine. There's a sushi bar, teppanyaki area for food cooked in the style of the Japanese steakhouse, and dining room, where such Japanese classics as tempura, teriyaki, katsu and sukiyaki are served. Lunch and dinner. Hamada's other locations offer varying degrees of service, and include spots at the Stratosphere, Flamingo, Rio, Luxor (sushi and dining room only), and Polo Towers (sushi and dining room only); plus Hamada Orient Express outlets at the MGM Grand, O'Shea's (also home to Hamada's Jay's Pizza), and Los Angeles International Airport. Hamada of Japan, 365 E. Flamingo Road; 702-733-3005 or www.hamadaofjapan.com.

So Hamada went to Kobe, and Ito taught his protégé the import-export business. He'd been working for Ito for a couple of years when Austin announced it was sending a group of executives on a tour that would include Kobe. Ito was eager to make a good impression. He'd send Hamada to dancing school. What Hamada didn't expect was that those lessons would last from 1 p.m. to 5 p.m. daily; Ito considered it part of his job. In the ensuing months, Hamada wore out several pairs of shoes.

By the time the Austin contingent arrived, Hamada could dance better than ever. He danced with the British ladies. The British ladies taught him to mambo. The Brits left, Hamada said, impressed with the strength of the Japanese culture only a few years after the war. Ito was happy. And he had another idea.

"He had the dream when he was young," Hamada said, of becoming a professional dancer. "He was 250 pounds." So his slight, agile student — Hamada remains that way 50 years later — would live his dream.

After about a year, the student was invited to join the Kondo Ballet School in Tokyo. Ito and his wife put their heads together. They discussed it with Hamada's father.

"Mr. Ito said, 'Congratulations, kid,'" Hamada remembered. "I said, 'Wait, what happened to my career?'" Ito offered to pay him the same salary to attend the school. "Why don't you go for it?" he remembered Ito saying. His mentor promised that Hamada could return to the import-export business in Kobe if things didn't work out in Tokyo. But things did work out. "I was told I was born to entertain the people," Hamada said. "All elements came together with the help of Mr. Ito."

Then in 1958 a representative from *The Ed Sullivan Show* was sent to find a team of Japanese cultural performers for a guest spot on the show. Hamada ended up as solo performer, choreographer, and producer of the *Japanese Festival Revue*. Today, he pulls out a photo of himself doing splits in the air. "I can't do that anymore," he said. He can, however, still do splits on the floor.

After his appearance on the TV show, Hamada traveled around the United States on tour for a year. He played the Desert Inn in Las Vegas. He played with Maurice Chevalier for a couple of months, and remembers him as "soft-spoken . . . that French accent. The way he danced. He was great."

He saw *West Side Story* — the memory still propels him into a burst of finger-snapping. He performed in *West Side Story* in Tokyo. The critics loved it, but Hamada was disappointed with show business in Japan. "They said it was a new style, but I said, no, it's a copy" of United States culture.

Besides, his thoughts were increasingly turning toward the real America. Back to Mr. Ito for advice. Ito encouraged the adventurer and offered to send him money. And if it didn't work out, always the promise, "Come back to Kobe."

Hamada shipped out — literally. He took a boat because "you can carry 10 Samsonites" and arrived in San Francisco on New Year's Eve 1962. He made his way to Las Vegas and worked for a few years,

mostly as a dishwasher and bartender and at one point selling Datsuns.

Then, in time-honored tradition, he took off for Europe in 1965 for more intensive study in the hospitality industry. Hamada got a six-month hotel management contract in Paris right away, and by the time he returned to the United States in 1971, he'd worked in 15 countries. He ended up with fluency in five languages — and a decided affection for Palatschinken, the Austrian crepe delicacy.

While he was in Europe, Hamada regularly showed up at American embassies, getting extensions to his green card. But after six years, immigration authorities decided he had studied enough. "After six years, they said, 'Tokyo or New York.'"

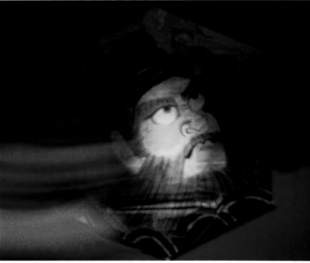

Las Vegas seemed like a more natural fit. He wouldn't have to return to primary school as he would if he wanted to settle in Switzerland, and he didn't feel the sting of discrimination in Las Vegas as he did in some parts of the United States.

"I must start from scratch," Hamada said. "I must find a place where I could start. I love this town — always so warm-hearted."

Back to Las Vegas, and in the next couple of years he held 12 jobs. "I was the first Oriental bartender at the El Cortez," he remembered with a twinkle.

"Then," he said, "I met Mr. Kerkorian." Kirk Kerkorian had owned the International, which

he had sold to Hilton in 1970, and still retained ties to the place. Hamada was hired to manage the Benihana at the Hilton. "Then my restaurant days began" in earnest, Hamada remembered. "So many people helped me."

He stayed at Benihana for three years, then moved on, managing restaurants at the Tropicana and the old Aladdin. He managed German and Italian restaurants, a steakhouse, a gourmet room. He thought about opening a restaurant, but couldn't find a suitable location.

And in the meantime, Hamada starting paying more attention to the city's visitors. "So many Japanese were in town," he noted. Surely they'd appreciate a travel service owned and operated by someone who understood their needs and spoke their language. "I must operate the No. 1 Japanese tour service in Las Vegas," he told himself. "Besides, the business license cost only $55."

In 1976, Hamada Travel Service was born. And Hamada decided it was time to go home for a visit. When he had left Japan to move to the United States, his father, from an old Samurai family, had told him not to come back until he was a success. So Hamada waited 15 years. When he went back, he said, his father asked, "What took you so long?"

He'd long dreamed of owning his own restaurant, and it seemed like a natural fit with the travel service. The first Hamada of Japan restaurant — on Flamingo Road just east of

Paradise Road, and east of the current location of the Hamada flagship — opened in 1987. "Then, my dream got started," Hamada said.

The restaurant's genesis was sort of the inverse of that of the tour service: Hamada realized all those Japanese visitors he was bringing in and touring around on buses needed a place to eat — a place that would feel like home. It was the Japanese equivalent of the American who seeks out a steak or a McDonald's in Europe or Asia, he said. "That was our bread and butter — the buses."

The tour service did well from the beginning, he said, and still exists, as Vegas Tour Service. He later hired someone to run it and is now a shareholder. But the restaurant just broke even for the first two years. And then in the third year, "bam, bang," he said. "I don't know why."

The "bam, bang" never stopped. Hamada now has nine restaurants — everything from his fine-dining places to Jay's Pizza at O'Shea's and Hamada Orient Express at Los Angeles International Airport. His newest restaurant, Hamada Asiana, opened at the Rio in April 2003.

Today, Hamada said, his key role is training — training the nearly 400 employees it takes to run his restaurants.

As for whether he plans to expand his empire further, he said, "I never think about tomorrow, just today. Maybe I'm

a gambler," but he's not talking about the tables. "I'm a gambler this way," he said, gesturing around his flagship.

Even the vagaries of business don't affect his irrepressible good humor. "I'm a lucky guy," Hamada said. "I've got lots of juice in Japan. Everybody knows Hamada in Vegas. I'm very happy."

Jay Hamada's

Sunomono (Cucumber Salad with Vinegar Dressing)

Sushi Rolls (Tuna)

Nigiri (Finger Sushi — Tuna, Whitefish, Salmon, and/or Shrimp)

Shrimp and Vegetable Tempura

Jay Hamada's

Sunomono

2 or 3 Japanese cucumbers
1 teaspoon salt
3 tablespoons rice wine vinegar
1 tablespoon sugar
1 teaspoon sesame seeds

Peel cucumbers and cut into thin slices. Sprinkle sliced cucumbers with salt and let stand for 5 minutes. Then squeeze out excess moisture.

For Dressing: Combine vinegar and sugar in a bowl and mix well. Pour the vinegar mixture over the cucumber slices and mix well. Serve in individual dishes; sprinkle sliced cucumbers with sesame seeds.

NOTE: You may add seaweed, crab, shrimp or other seafood.

Serves 4 to 6.

Jay Hamada's

Sushi Rolls and Nigiri Sushi

For Sushi Rolls:
1 package nori (toasted seaweed sheets)
½ recipe prepared Sushi Rice (recipe follows)
About 6 to 8 ounces sushi-grade tuna

For Nigiri Sushi:
About 8 ounces sushi-grade tuna,
whitefish, salmon, or cooked shrimp
Wasabi
½ recipe prepared Sushi Rice (recipe follows)

For Sushi Rice:
2 cups uncooked sushi rice
5 tablespoons rice vinegar
2 teaspoons sugar
½ teaspoon salt
¼ cup mirin (Japanese sweet rice wine)

Sushi Rolls: For each roll, take a sheet of toasted seaweed and break or cut in half.

Put a half sheet of seaweed on a makisu (bamboo rolling mat), and place a handful of cool vinegared rice on the seaweed. Distribute rice evenly, then pat down gently so rice sticks to the seaweed.

Lay four strips of tuna (about ½ ounce each) on the center of the rice. Draw the seaweed up so the two long sides meet, forming a roll. Wrap the makisu around the rough roll and press, to condense the roll and make it stay rolled.

Remove makisu. Slice the roll in half, creating two short rolls. Slice each short roll into 3 pieces — creating six slices per roll. Repeat until fish and rice are used up.

Refrigerate until time to serve.

Serves 4 to 6.

Nigiri Sushi: Slice the fish of your choice into bite-sized pieces. Dab a small amount of wasabi on one side of the fish.

Take about 2 tablespoons of cooked sushi rice and shape into a firm ball. Press the fish, wasabi-side down, onto the rice. Gently hand-sculpt it into an oblong; press down again with the index and middle fingers. The rice has to be tight enough to hold a shape, but loose enough to melt in your mouth. Refrigerate until time to serve.

Serves 4 to 6.

Sushi rice: Rinse uncooked rice repeatedly under cold water until water runs clear; drain. Soak rinsed rice with fresh water until it reaches the first knuckle of your index finger (knuckle nearest your palm). Cook in a rice cooker; when rice is done, let it sit for 15 minutes.

While the rice is in the cooker, place a saucepan over moderate heat and add the vinegar, sugar, salt, and mirin.

When the rice is cooked, and still hot, combine with liquid in a bowl. Let rice cool.

Jay Hamada's

Shrimp and Vegetable Tempura

For Shrimp and Vegetable Tempura:
Vegetable oil
½ pound tiger shrimp, cleaned, tails on
Flour
1 cup broccoli florets
1 sweet potato, peeled and sliced ¼-inch thick
1 cup zucchini, sliced ¼-inch thick
1 large onion, peeled and cut ¼-inch thick

For Tempura Batter:
1 egg yolk
1 cup cold water
1 cup tempura flour

For Tempura Sauce:
½ cup mirin (Japanese sweet rice wine)
½ cup light soy sauce
1 teaspoon sugar
¼ cup grated daikon radish

Shrimp And Vegetable Tempura: Heat the vegetable oil to 375 ° F in a wok or deep fryer. Prepare vegetables and dry well. Dust shrimp in flour to soak up remaining moisture; shake off excess.

Prepare tempura batter and sauce.

Dip the shrimp and vegetables into the batter one by one and carefully place in oil to fry. Fry until golden brown, turning once, about 3 to 4 minutes. Remove from oil and drain on paper towels. Serve with dipping sauce.

Serves 4 to 6.

For Tempura Batter: In a mixing bowl, lightly beat egg yolk and pour in water until slightly mixed. Add the flour all at once; stroke a few times with a fork just until ingredients are loosely combined. Batter should be somewhat lumpy.

Tempura Sauce: In a small saucepan over low heat, combine mirin, soy sauce, and sugar. Cook for 3 to 5 minutes, until sugar dissolves. Transfer to individual bowl. Add grated radish just before serving.

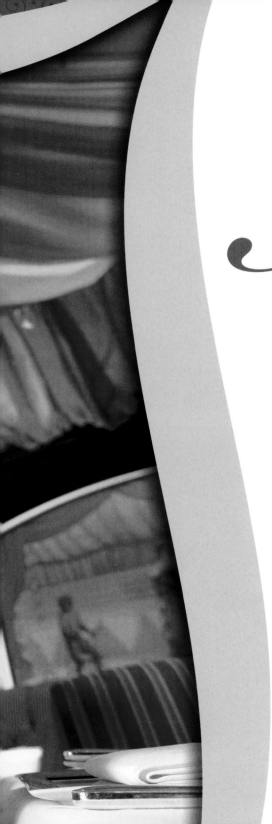

Marc Poidevin

Le Cirque

"I am determined to not be a big sparkle in the middle of the fireworks — and then, poof!"

For Marc Poidevin, culinary school was a starting point. "After that," he said, "you put on your own toque and become what you become."

What Poidevin has become is one of the top chefs in the country, and executive chef at Le Cirque and Osteria del Circo, both at Bellagio. And far from being formed of whole cloth, his career has been woven of bits and pieces that include a stint at the French presidential palace and a trip through a "killing field" in New York.

Poidevin was born in Montauban, France — in the same state as Alain Ducasse, now widely considered one of the world's best chefs. "We grew up in that same sort of environment, eating the same food," Poidevin said. That would be hearty, classic French fare, with cassoulets, foie gras, truffles, duck, and goose playing starring roles. Poidevin's exposure to such food was particularly up close and personal, as his parents owned a charcuterie, dealing in cured and prepared meats.

At 14, he entered culinary school in Toulouse. Poidevin says the school was one of the best in France, and it would certainly expand his horizons. He learned about fish — not a big item in land-locked Montauban — and "a little bit of everything," particularly during the first year, when students worked in the kitchen and dining room and studied

enology, sanitation, and hotel management. It was a boarding school and the schedule wasn't easy — six days a week, starting class at 8 a.m. and into the kitchen by 2 p.m. "I did the dining room, but that was not what attracted me the most," Poidevin said. No, that was "definitely on the line, in the back."

Looking back, Poidevin remains impressed with the quality of his instructors. "They were all top of the line," he said, averaging 20 to 30 years in the trenches. "They were very, very experienced people."

Second-year students concentrated on specific areas of interest, which in Poidevin's case was cooking. The third year was a sort of externship, in which students remained loosely connected to the school. "They like to keep an eye on you at least a year after," he said, "until you fly on your own wings."

Poidevin took his first job when one of his instructors invited him to go along with him to Copenhagen for the summer season at a private club. "I said, 'Why not?'" He'd learn a lot more about fish, as it was the featured entrée at dinner each evening.

He moved on to a 1930s-era hotel in the embassy district of Copenhagen with,

Poidevin remembered, "an amazing view of the ocean — very, very pretty neighborhood." And he'd learn even more about fish, including how to cure gravlax. "They have an amazing technique over there," he said. "What they do with salmon is amazing."

He also was able to visit small processors where fish was smoked, and remembered a lovely smoked halibut that was yellow on top and snow-white on the bottom. "The flavor is extraordinary," Poidevin said. "It's something you only find over there."

L e Cirque, an outpost of the famed Le Cirque 2000 in New York, is one of the most expensive restaurants in Las Vegas — and also one of the least pretentious. The ceiling is tented with silk to invoke the spirit of a big old-fashioned circus tent, but this is an elegant, intimate space with accents of magenta and gold. And if the overseas tourist perched next to you on one of Le Cirque's plush banquettes should happen to order a Budweiser, the waiter will hesitate not a whit before fetching a cold bottle, pouring it carefully into stemmed sparkling crystal and presenting it with aplomb, much as he'd serve one of Le Cirque's $12,000 bottles. When he creates his daily menu, Marc Poidevin updates and interprets the best of his native France, offering such dishes as a risotto with morels and a roasted duck breast and confit leg with spring vegetables. Dinner only. Next door to Le Cirque is Osteria del Circo, a more casual — and larger — restaurant with a Tuscan flavor, where Poidevin also presides. Le Cirque, Bellagio, 3600 Las Vegas Blvd. South, 702-693-7223 or www.bellagio.com.

His next move was to Luxembourg, to a Michelin two-star restaurant whose chef had been sous chef to French culinary icon Roger Verge. "I started to work with incredible things," imported from all over, Poidevin said. "It was a very provençal style of cooking, but with a huge variety of product."

The kitchen was "very, very French," he said, with little communication among the staff. "It was like the orchestra," he said, with the chef as conductor. There was a new menu every day, and so much to learn. Poidevin remembered working 18 hours a day, six days a week. "Otherwise, there was no way to get my head out of the water," he said. Lunch was grabbed on the run — which kept Poidevin at 110 pounds, wearing pants with a 28-inch waist. And the exacting organizational habits he'd acquired in culinary school were honed further.

"There was no waiting at the pass," Poidevin said. "Stuff is coming out from all different stations." Each employee had to be Johnny-on-the-spot; "otherwise you disrupt the entire kitchen. If you went from your station to the garde manger, you'd better have a good reason. If there's one ingredient missing in the sauce, the chef will find it right away." Said Poidevin, in what appeared to be supreme understatement: "It was very, very intense."

Still, he stuck it out for a year and a half, and then moved on to the Michelin three-star Moulin de Mougin, near Cannes, which Poidevin said is "one of the prettiest places in France." And the restaurant was one of the best, the chef another Verge protégé. "Name one major chef in France, they all went through the kitchen," Poidevin said.

During the Cannes Film Festival, the restaurant was inundated with celebrities — good training for Poidevin's future jobs with Le Cirque. He also was able to find time for a little fun. "We kind of had a good time between midnight and 3 in the morning."

But America beckoned: Poidevin was asked to help open a restaurant at the Hotel Westbury in New York City, and worked there as a pastry chef with Daniel Bóulud, Thomas Keller, and Alfred Portale— only to be called back to France for his compulsory military service. In the service he would have it better than many; after three months of training on the Atlantic coast, Poidevin was assigned to what he calls "the White House" — the French presidential palace, the Elysee. There was served "traditional French cuisine — very formal," he remembered. Among the dinner guests: Ronald Reagan and Mikhail Gorbachev.

The hours were better — "not as intense as working in a three-star restaurant," he said. And so Poidevin, accustomed to working almost continuously, did a little moonlighting in a Michelin two-star in Paris.

When he slept is uncertain, because he was spending his nights at the Rungis wholesale market outside the city, where he "saw amazing things. It's a city outside Paris — a city of food," he said, still registering wide-eyed amazement. He got along well with the sous chef at the Elysee, so he was able to take the presidential car to the market "and buy whatever I wanted — I didn't even look at the price. My life was really, really good."

After his year of service was up, it was back to the United States and the Plaza Athenee in New York, in 1983. A year later, he moved to the original Le Cirque on 65th Street. It was quite a team: Poidevin and rising stars Sottha Khun and Bóulud.

"He took the whole package from the Plaza Athenee," Poidevin said of Le Cirque owner Sirio Maccioni. "We were young. The energy was there." Then fellow rising star Jacques Torres joined the team, and "the pastry did a big high 360 in the air," Poidevin said.

Plaudits followed; a year and a half after the young chefs came on board, Le Cirque got four stars from the New York Times. But soon Poidevin would decide to move on again — this time to Maxim de Paris. "After a year or two, there was not enough action for me," he said.

Oh, how that would change on his next move. In May 1989, Poidevin got a call from Walker LeRoy, owner of Tavern on the Green in New York. He wanted action? He'd get action. At Tavern on the Green, the kitchen served 2,500 meals a night.

"It was a humongous place," Poidevin said. And LeRoy, he said, was "very impulsive. We did have a couple of fights in the kitchen." Poidevin was in his late 20s then, and "at

the time I was very hyper, very energetic." Good thing. "It was like the war on the front line." It also was, Poidevin said, the highest-paying chef's job in the country. "The money they were putting on the table, it was hard to say no." On the other hand, "Every penny they pay you, you earn it."

He said he didn't see the sun for three months at a time. "I felt like I was in Alaska." He had a three-year contract, and then agreed to two one-year extensions, staying five years in total. "I think I'm in the *Guinness Book of Records*," he quipped.

"The problem was, they couldn't find anybody to replace me. Nobody in New York wanted to touch that place because it was the killing field. You have to be very strong physically to run a place like that, because it's the New York marathon."

He was young and strong, but after five years, he'd had enough. By 1995, he said, "I was kind of burned out. I exiled myself for a year. I needed time physically and mentally to rebuild myself." What better place for an escape than a tropical island? Poidevin went to the Caribbean for almost a year. But "after nine months, I was really bored."

His dream had been to open a restaurant "with the heart and soul of a real French brasserie," and he was about to get his chance. Real-estate magnate Don Sofer, a friend of Maccioni, was planning just such a project in Miami. Poidevin opened The Big Bistro at Aventura Mall and stayed

there for about a year, but he'd heard that Le Cirque, shuttered for renovations, was about to re-open as Le Cirque 2000 in a new location, with Sottha Khun as chef. Poidevin jumped. "I was with Sottha again," he said — "Frick and Frack again."

Two years later, Khun was getting ready to move on, and Steve Wynn wanted to open a Le Cirque in his new Bellagio. "A small dining room, 70 seats. Ooh, I like that," Poidevin remembered thinking. "Obviously, the budget was high. He said he wanted to have the best restaurant in Las Vegas, which at the time was not too difficult."

"I came here, looked at the place. I looked at Vegas, the lifestyle, the whole package." It was important that his wife and three sons thought they could be happy living in Las Vegas.

Poidevin's choice was to be executive chef at Le Cirque 2000 in New York, "or start something new from scratch. The guys in the kitchen said they'd come — two or three of the major guys. I looked at what the team would look like. At least I'm not alone. Then after, we can build on that."

Le Cirque at Bellagio opened October 15, 1998. At first, Poidevin said, he felt smothered by the Bellagio hierarchy; he said at least one other Bellagio chef felt the same way. "We wanted to keep our identity," he said. "At the beginning, it was not easy."

But almost five years later, Poidevin still is energized by Le Cirque. "I'm a chef, and I'm

still in the kitchen most of the time," he said. He experiments with food during the early morning; "at 11, the phone starts to ring."

Poidevin stays true to his roots, for instance using truffles and other foods of his youth whenever possible. His menus are "very seasonal. I always get the first of the season," he said. "That's essential for me, and my suppliers know it."

"I think my food is very, very basic," he said. "I come from a very traditional training." He likes to emphasize the sensory aspects of food as well as the flavor, "but not too complex." With some chefs, he said, "at the end, you don't know what you're eating anymore." Honoring culinary traditions, he said, is "a very difficult thing to do. Everybody can do lobster. A pig foot — that's a tough thing to do."

And he wants his customers to know what to expect. "Consistency for me is a very, very important thing," Poidevin said. He's focusing on developing local clientele and repeat business. But he's finding that at the same time, Le Cirque is drawing lots of Europeans. "That, for me, is a very positive thing."

In the meantime, his goal is to attain Mobil five-star and AAA five-diamond status for Le Cirque. "I am determined," he said, "to not be a big sparkle in the middle of the fireworks — and then, poof!"

Marc Poidevin's

PERSONAL FAVORITES

Roasted Monkfish Medallion with Crayfish Tails

French White Asparagus
"Des Landes" Gratineed with Parmesan

Braised Veal Shank

Marc Poidevin's

Roasted Monkfish Medallion
with Crayfish Tails, Potato and Celery Root Galette

4 boneless monkfish tails (cleaned
and formed into a cylinder)
6 tablespoons clarified butter
(divided use)
4 cloves garlic, crushed
4 sprigs thyme
4 ounces crayfish tails (poached
and de-veined)
Olive oil
8 ounces Vermouth and Fines
Herbs Sauce (recipe follows)
Potato and Celery Root Galette
(recipe follows)
2 ounces Crayfish Butter
(recipe follows)

Vermouth and Fines Herb Sauce
1 pound monkfish bones
Olive oil
4 shallots
1 onion
1 fennel bulb
2 carrots
1 rib celery
1 head garlic
Sachet of thyme, bay leaf,
coriander, fennel
seed, and peppercorns, gathered
into a square of
cheesecloth and tied

1 cup vermouth
2 cups white wine
1 gallon chicken stock
Heavy cream
½ pound butter
Fines herbs:
1 tablespoon tarragon
1 tablespoon chervil
1 tablespoon flat leaf parsley
1 tablespoon chives

Potato and Celery Root Galette
4 medium Yukon Gold potatoes
1 medium-sized celery root
Salt
Pepper
1 tablespoon clarified butter

Crayfish Butter
1 pound crayfish shells
1 pound shrimp shells
5 heads garlic
1 teaspoon rosemary
1 teaspoon thyme
½ cup butter

Monkfish medalions: Preheat oven to 400° F. Place monkfish tails in pan with 2 tablespoons smoking hot clarified butter and place in oven for 3 minutes. Remove pan from oven and turn fish. Add 4 tablespoons clarified butter, crushed garlic cloves, and thyme. Baste the fish with the foaming butter mixture several times and return to oven. After an additional 3 minutes, check for doneness.

Crayfish tails: Sauté crayfish in hot pan with olive oil; remove from flame and add vermouth sauce.

To serve: Place potato and celery root galette on each plate, topped by crayfish tails and the monkfish fillet. Spoon vermouth sauce around and drizzle crayfish butter over to finish.

Serves 4.

Vermouth and Fines Herb Sauce: In large Dutch oven or heavy saucepan, roast fish bones in olive oil until golden brown on all sides. Add vegetables and sachet and cook gently, without browning, just until translucent. Remove sachet.

De-glaze pan with vermouth and scrape to remove any stuck-on particles; cook until alcohol has evaporated. De-glaze with white wine and reduce by half; cover bones with chicken stock and simmer for ½ hour.

Pass broth through sieve and swirl in a splash of heavy cream and cold diced butter; season to taste.

Finely chop fines herbs and add before serving.

NOTE: Leftover sauce may be frozen for another use.

Potato and Celery Root Galette: Boil potatoes for 15 to 20 minutes until 75 percent cooked.

Peel potatoes and celery root and shave on a box grater into a large bowl. Mix with salt, pepper and clarified butter. Divide mixture into four portions and place in a small, buttered, nonstick pan. Cook until golden brown on both sides.

Crayfish Butter: Pulverize all ingredients in stand mixer with paddle attachment.

Place mixture in heavy-bottomed Dutch oven or large skillet and place in 300° F oven for 2 hours, stirring occasionally. Strain butter through cheesecloth and season with salt and pepper.

Marc Poidevin's

French White Asparagus "Des Landes" Gratineed with Parmesan, Warm Goat Cheese Croutons, and Mache Salad

24 pieces white asparagus "des landes"
(or jumbo green asparagus)
1 round of Crottin de Chavignol goat cheese
4 slices ciabatta (Italian peasant bread)
2 tablespoons balsamic vinegar
4 ounces Plugra butter
Salt and pepper to taste
1 tablespoon sherry vinegar
½ cup Parmesan cheese, grated
¼ pound baby mache, cleaned

Peel asparagus and cook in boiling salted water until just crisp-tender; remove and plunge into ice water.

Slice goat cheese and place on top of slices of ciabatta.

To make dressing: heat balsamic vinegar in a small saucepan and reduce to a syrupy consistency. Brown butter over medium heat until golden and add to balsamic vinegar; add seasoning and sherry vinegar.

To serve: Lay asparagus on buttered sizzle platter and sprinkle with Parmesan cheese; heat under broiler until golden brown.

Place goat cheese croutons in 400° F oven until cheese is melted.

Place asparagus gratin on plate atop mache.

Place crouton to the side and season with balsamic dressing.

Serves 4.

Marc Poidevin's

Braised Veal Shank
with Lemon, Cumin, and Glazed Root Vegetables

1 veal shank
Salt
Pepper
Flour
Olive oil
1 onion, diced
1 carrot, diced
1 stalk celery, diced
4 shallots, chopped
1 head garlic, minced
Sachet of cumin, coriander, cardamom
peppercorns, and lemon zest, gathered into a
square of cheesecloth and tied
10 sprigs thyme
4 plum tomatoes, quartered and seeded

2 cups white wine
1 quart chicken stock
1 quart veal stock
Glazed Root Vegetables (recipe follows)
Lemon Chips (recipe follows)

For vegetables:
1 daikon
8 baby turnips
8 baby carrots
1 piece celery root
4 Yukon Gold potatoes
Veal shank sauce from previous recipe

For tomato confit:
4 plum tomatoes
Sea salt to taste
Thyme to taste
Lemon peel to taste
Olive oil to taste

For mushrooms:
4 ounces oyster mushrooms
Clarified butter
Salt and pepper to taste
Parsley

For: Lemon Chips
1 lemon
1 ounce powdered sugar

Season shank with salt and pepper, dust with flour, and sear in olive oil in heavy-bottomed pan. Add onion, carrot, celery, shallots, garlic, sachet, and thyme and cook until vegetables are translucent without allowing mixture to brown. Add tomatoes and cook down to remove water. Remove sachet.

Add wine and scrape up any bits adhering to pan. Cook down by half. Add chicken and veal stocks to barely cover. Simmer for 1 ½ t o 2 hours, until tender.

Remove meat from bone and roll in plastic wrap to form a tight cylinder. Place in ice bath to firm. When cold, slice thin.

Strain sauce and reduce, then season and add olive oil to taste. Return thinly sliced shank to sauce and glaze in oven.

Assembly: Place glazed veal shank in center of plate. Position glazed root vegetables around veal. Top with crispy oyster mushrooms and tomato confit. Spoon sauce around and drizzle extra-virgin olive oil over top. Place lemon chip on top.

Serves 4.

For vegetables: Pare daikon, turnips, carrots, celery root, and potatoes into shapes similar to a football and braise in veal shank sauce until cooked.

For tomato confit: Blanch and skin tomatoes and cut them in half. Sprinkle with sea salt, thyme, lemon peel, and olive oil and roast at 150° F for 5 to 6 hours.

For oyster mushrooms: Sauté in clarified butter until crispy and season with salt, pepper, and parsley.

Serves 4.

Lemon Chips: Slice lemon in half and remove seeds. Slice paper-thin and toss in powdered sugar. Place on non-stick sheet in a 250° F oven for 2 hours, or until crisp. Remove from oven and place in cool dry place.

Michael Mina

Nobhill

"I always wore whites. I was always in the kitchen for lunch and dinner. It's definitely the part of the job I enjoy the most. By far."

Michael Mina's early culinary training echoes that of European chefs for generations before his. But while most who follow his path were born in France or other parts of Western Europe and entered time-honored apprenticeship programs on the European continent, Mina was a kid from Egypt whose baptism-by-fire took place in a small town in Washington state.

Mina, who was born in Cairo, said his parents decided to leave Egypt when he, the youngest of their three children, was a year old. "My family was Christian, and they thought it would be best for the kids if we left," he said.

They moved to Ellensburg, Washington, where his father took a job at Central Washington University. The Egyptian language was spoken in the family home and Mina remains fluent, although he speaks unaccented English.

But in every other way he was the typical small-town American boy. Basketball was a passion, and "I was pretty talented at the time," he said. He pursued the game enthusiastically; maybe some day, he'd be a star.

Mina's coach, however, seemed to have other ideas, which may have stemmed

It seems most people go to Nobhill for the sourdough — or maybe the lobster pot pie — but it's a good bet a lot of them return for the five flavors of mashed potatoes, served all at once in what feels like an embarrassment of riches. Nobhill's location off the casino, near the front desk, is away from the MGM Grand's restaurant row. Its dining room is sleek and airy, but if you're smart you'll reserve one of the intimate booths near the restaurant's entrance, each with its own San Francisco address. The sourdough is as fragrant and crusty as though baked in the Bay Area just hours before, and it's served in a silver basket atop a punched-metal light/warmer; as the entrees are served, the bread is set aside to make way for the mashed potatoes, in flavors that might include lobster, curry, mushroom, horseradish, and basil. Cheese fondue is a cozy, creamy wonder, foie gras a rich indulgence, and everything is served in the highest style. Dinner only. Michael Mina has two other Las Vegas restaurants — Michael Mina Bellagio and Seablue at the MGM Grand. Nobhill, MGM Grand, 3799 Las Vegas Blvd. South; 702-891-7337 or www.mgmgrand.com.

from some bias against his foreign-born player. The teen felt he wasn't being given as many opportunities as some of the other players, and wanted to quit the team. "But with my dad, you don't quit something in the middle," Mina said. Son persisted; Dad was adamant. Wanna quit? Dad asked. Get a job. "So that's what I did," Mina said.

A friend's father was looking for help. The man owned a small French restaurant, and brought Mina in as a fledgling garde-manger in the three-person kitchen. And there Mina discovered something he liked as much as shooting hoops.

"I was very much into it," he said. He especially liked the adrenaline rush that rises from the steam in a restaurant kitchen, with its characteristically breakneck pace. "The stress and the pressure," Mina said with a trace of amusement. "Now that's the part I hate the most."

The pressure was only beginning. When Mina was 16, his friend's father fell ill. It was up to Mina to run the restaurant, which he did during his junior and senior years of high school. His innovative streak came through from the outset. "You tried to do nice things for the time," Mina said. He'd get up in the morning and go to school, until his classes ended at 10:30 a.m. "Then I'd go to work. Work lunch, work dinner, close the restaurant. It was fun. It was like a big party."

Besides cooking, he managed the place for the owner. "He paid me pretty well for being that young," Mina remembered. He spent three and half years there, running the restaurant for the last two. And by age 17 he knew he wanted to go to cooking school.

But Mina's father, who was the president of the business department at Central Washington, wasn't pleased, and suggested his son try a conventional college first. Mina took classes at the University of Washington for one quarter, "and all I did was complain about school," he said. And he couldn't stay out of the kitchen. He also was working in a restaurant in the Seattle Space Needle.

Eventually, Mina's father relented: He could go to culinary school. But when this young man who'd been in love with San Francisco ever since seeing a picture of the Golden Gate Bridge as a child applied to the California Culinary Academy in the Bay Area, he was rejected. (And today, "Every time I teach a course there, I let them know," he said with a quiet chuckle.) The Culinary Institute of America had better judgment. Mina left for Hyde Park, New York. And he was no longer complaining about school. "I thought the school was great," he said of the CIA.

He did a six-month externship with George Morrone, then executive chef at the Hotel Bel-Air in Southern California. And he spent weekends working with respected chef Charlie Palmer in New York. "Aureole was just opening, and it was the hot place in New York," Mina remembered.

After graduation, he returned to Los Angeles to work again for Morrone. It was shortly thereafter that Mina and Morrone met Charles Condy, who had a business proposition for a restaurant. In San Francisco.

"We realized there was no really great fish restaurant in San Francisco," Mina said. "There should be. I think we just kind of hit that right on stride." The restaurant would be Aqua, one of the best seafood restaurants American foodies had ever experienced. "We were always true to the concept," Mina said. "We saw a niche and filled it. It was exactly the right timing. San Francisco was ready for that experience," the same way Aureole struck a chord in New York.

And Aqua paid other dividends. "It was a very enjoyable restaurant to be a chef of," Mina said. In the Bay Area, "there's an endless supply of fish. Most of it's cooked to order. It's a fun kitchen environment to work in — high pressure." Mina said he especially had an affinity for the energy of Aqua. "I like being associated with restaurants that have life in them," he said. He said he viewed any restaurant as equal parts food, service, and atmosphere. Aqua, he said, is "very sophisticated, upscale, but still pleasant and fun."

Of his restaurants, Mina said, "They're all close to your heart in one way or another." He later opened Aqua, later renamed Michael Mina Bellagio, at the Bellagio in Las Vegas, but he also is especially fond of Nobhill at the MGM Grand. "Nobhill's one of my absolute favorites," Mina said. He said he viewed it as upscale and sophisticated, but that the visible bread oven and mashed-potato service help instill a homey feel. He said he also thinks the staff is truly in tune with what he's trying to accomplish.

And Nobhill, he said, was the first restaurant for which he got to work on the design. "We worked on this together from start to finish," he said as he gazed around the darkened restaurant a few hours before service was to begin.

Nobhill's place in his heart may have something to do with the way Mina feels about Las Vegas. "I love Las Vegas," he said. "People said it would be hard to find staff and you're gonna hate the clientele. It was just the opposite, in both cases. What better clientele than 200 to 300 people walking in your door every night and they're looking to have a good time?"

Mina's relationship with Condy and the Aqua Development Group would come to an end, in large part because of differing philosophies. Mina and Condy parted ways late in 2002, after which Mina formed the Mina Group. Andre Agassi is a principal; Mina said he's "a good friend and regular customer." In Las Vegas Mina has Michael Mina Bellagio, Seablue, and Nobhill at MGM.

But despite the parting of the ways, Mina said he's grateful for the time he spent in business with Condy. "It was a valuable learning experience," he said. "We opened eight restaurants and I operated as an executive chef and president of the company" — and, in finest Michael Mina tradition, at a young age; he was only 34 when he split with Condy. "I got to work with some of the very best people in the industry."

So instead of looking back, he's looking ahead. New projects since he split with Condy include the Michael Mina Restaurant at the St. Francis Hotel in San Francisco and Seablue, which features interactive cooking within the dining room and is "straightforward — very approachable." Like other chefs who are considered industry leaders, he sees the importance of a back-to-basics, "back-to-product" movement in the restaurant industry.

He's considering a children's cooking show, adding that "that's the only show I really want to do." The purpose, he said, would be to teach parents how to work with their children in the kitchen. He's had quite a bit of experience in that himself, regularly cooking with his two young sons, Sammy and Anthony, and says the experience has especially brought him closer to Sammy, his older son.

Mina remains philosophical about his growing status as a celebrity chef. "My early start helped," he said. "Aqua was a good showcase. But you are only as good as the people who work for you. You have to do everything in your power to keep the right people."

He said he still tries to get into the kitchen every day. At Aqua in San Francisco, he said, "I always wore whites. I was always in the kitchen for lunch and dinner. It's definitely the part of the job I enjoy the most. By far."

♣

ENTREES

BUTTER POACHED OREGON SALMON
Hobb's Smoked Bacon, Creamy Lentils, Soft

NORTH BEACH CIOPPINO
Assorted Seasonal Shellfish, Spicy Tomato Bro

MICHAEL'S LOBSTER POT PIE
2-Pound Maine Lobster, Baby Winter Vegetables

ROASTED YOUNG SONOMA CHICKEN
Truffled Macaroni & Cheese, Organic Broccoli, Cr

WOOD GRILLED DIVER SCALLOPS
to Gnocchi, Red Onion Comp

POMEGRANAT
ith

Michael Mina's

PERSONAL FAVORITES

*Seared Scallop and Organic Watercress Salad
with White Corn Pudding and Truffle Vinaigrette*

*Grilled Amish Chicken
with Truffled Macaroni and Cheese*

*Fresh Fruit Tart Tatin
with Tahitian Vanilla Bean Ice Cream*

Michael Mina's

Seared Scallop and Organic Watercress Salad with White Corn Pudding and Truffle Vinaigrette

1 cup white corn juice (use a vegetable juicer)
1 tablespoon truffle vinegar
1 tablespoon sherry vinegar
1 medium shallot, minced
1 tablespoon extra-virgin olive oil
1 tablespoon truffle oil
¼ cup grapeseed or canola oil
1 tablespoon chives, finely chopped
8 1-ounce sea scallops
Salt and black pepper
4 teaspoons clarified butter or vegetable oil
4 ounces organic watercress

To make the corn pudding: simmer the corn juice in a saucepan over medium heat. Whisk the juice constantly until it thickens; this happens instantaneously. Remove the corn pudding from the heat and set aside.

To make the vinaigrette: combine the vinegars and minced shallot in a mixing bowl. Whisk in the olive, truffle and grapeseed or canola oils. Add chopped chives and season to taste.

Season the scallops on both sides with salt and pepper. Sear the scallops in a medium sauté pan using the clarified butter or vegetable oil. Once the scallops are caramelized on both sides, remove them from the pan and place on a plate layered with a paper towel. Using a round plate, spoon two dollops of corn pudding, spaced a few inches apart, on the plate. Place a scallop on top of each dollop.

Toss the watercress in the truffle vinaigrette and season. Do not overdress the watercress or it will wilt and lose its crisp texture. The watercress salad goes between the scallops. Garnish the plate with the remaining vinaigrette.

Serves 4.

Michael Mina's

Grilled Amish Chicken
with Truffled Macaroni And Cheese

1 pound macaroni
4 Amish chicken thighs (or other chicken)
Salt
Black pepper
Flour for dusting
2 tablespoons canola oil
1 yellow onion, sliced
2 garlic cloves, smashed
½ bunch thyme
4 cups chicken stock
2 cups heavy cream
4 ounces grated Parmesan or Asiago cheese
4 to 6 ounces white truffle oil (available at
specialty supermarkets)
4 Amish chicken breasts (or other chicken;
boneless skinless can be used if preferred)
1 head broccoli, steamed

For macaroni and cheese: In a large pot of salted boiling water, cook macaroni as per the instructions on the package. Meanwhile, remove the skin from the chicken thighs. Season well with salt and pepper, then dust with flour. Heat oil over medium heat in a heavy-bottomed pot (a straight-sided saute pan with a 3-quart or greater capacity would be best).

Place the dusted thighs in the pot, turning once when browned, about 3 to 4 minutes. When the thighs are browned on both sides, remove and set on the side (they will not be fully cooked at this point).

Add the sliced onion, garlic, and thyme to the pan and cook for about 4 to 5 minutes, or until the onions are transluscent. Add the chicken stock to the pan and bring to a simmer, scraping the bottom of the pan to remove any browned bits. When the stock has reached a simmer, return the thighs to the pan and simmer for 5 to 8 minutes, or until the thighs are fully cooked. Remove the thighs and set aside to cool.

Whisk in cream and let simmer for 3 to 5 minutes. Strain and whisk in the cheese while the sauce is still warm. Season to taste and set aside.

Once the thighs have cooled, pick the meat from the bones, removing any fat or gristle. Stir meat into the sauce. At this point, the sauce and macaroni can be combined over medium heat. Before you serve, stir in the truffle oil.

For chicken breast: Season the chicken well with salt and pepper. Grill over medium heat for about 6 to 8 minutes, turning often.

Serve with steamed broccoli florets that have been tossed in butter, salt, and pepper.

Serves 4.

Michael Mina's

Fresh Fruit Tart Tatin
with Tahitian Vanilla Bean Ice Cream

½ cup cream
½ cup milk
¾ cup sugar
Pinch of salt
1 vanilla bean
11 egg yolks
10 tablespoons butter
1 tablespoon lemon juice
1 ¾ cups, plus 2 tablespoons sugar
Fresh ripe fruit of your choice
Frozen puff pastry, thawed

To make ice cream: bring cream, milk, sugar, salt and vanilla bean to a boil.

Whisk yolks in a bowl, then whisk in a little of the hot mixture, and finally mix yolks into remaining cream mixture. Cook ice cream base over low heat until it coats the back of a spoon (when you run your finger across the back of the spoon, the mixture should not flow back together).

Strain through a chinois or other fine strainer into a bowl. Place bowl immediately into an ice bath until cool, stirring occasionally. When ice-cream base is cold, process in an ice-cream machine.

To make caramel: melt butter in a saucepan. Add lemon juice and sugar, and stir just until combined. Cook over medium-high heat until it reaches a nice caramel color (don't let it get too dark, as it will continue to darken as you pull it off the heat).

To assemble: preheat oven to 375° F. Ladle or pour the caramel just to cover the bottom of an 8-inch cake pan. Once the caramel is set, slice your desired fruit evenly and arrange neatly in pan on top of caramel.

Cut the pastry to cover the top of pan. (Keep in mind puff pastry shrinks as you bake it, so you can cut it a little bigger then the actual size of the pan.) Bake tart in oven until puff pastry is risen and golden brown.

Remove from oven, place a plate over the pan and with two towels flip the tart over. Serve warm with the ice cream.

Serves 6 to 8.

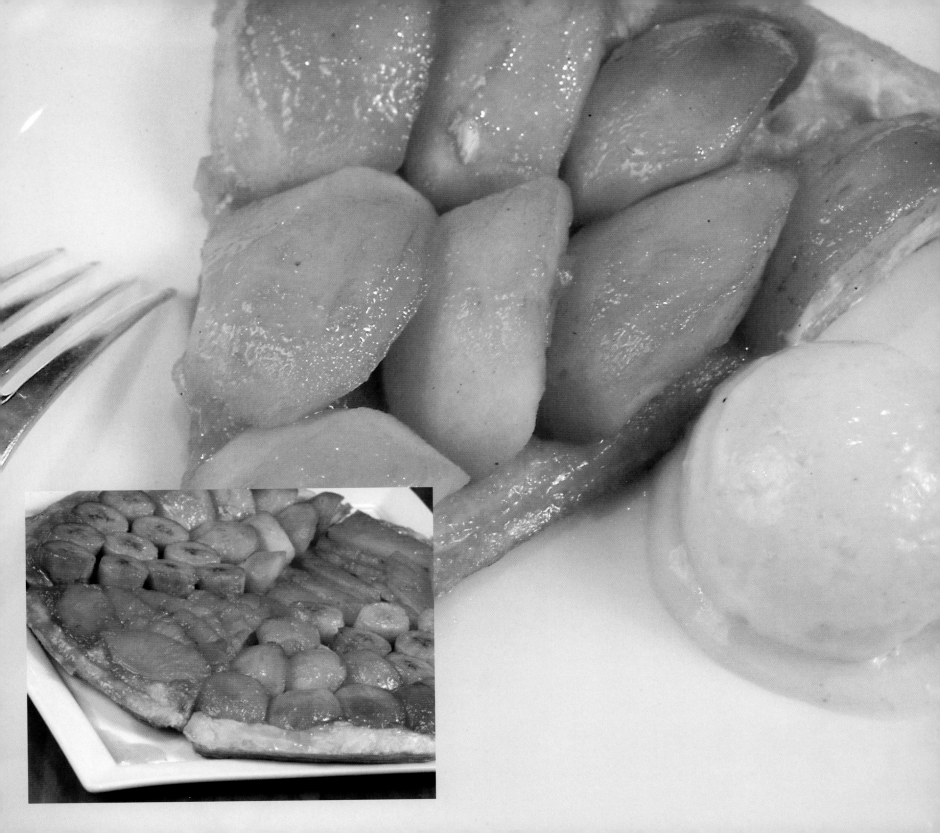

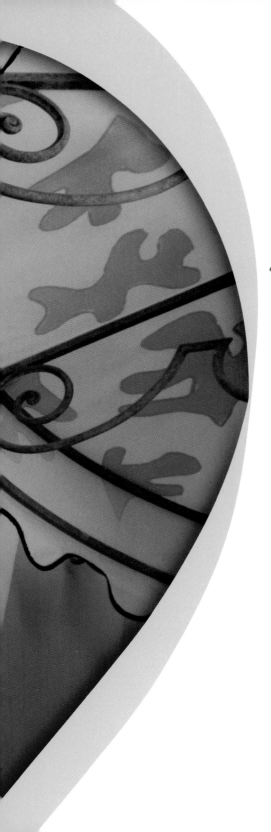

Todd English

Olives

"Let's not talk about recipes. Let's talk about cooking. The difference is the feeling."

Todd English is a chef-businessman with more than a dozen restaurants across the country. But for English, it's not about the money, and it's not about the fame. It's about the food. "My juices," he said, "start flowing when I can touch it."

You want to chat with English about the inspiration for his recipes? "Let's not talk about recipes," he said. "Let's talk about cooking. The difference is the feeling."

English does indeed like to talk about cooking, and it was ever thus. He was born in Amarillo, Texas, but grew up in various parts of the country as his father pursued a broadcasting career. English's mother is an accomplished cook, and it was in her kitchen that he got his

start. By age 7 or 8 he was selling sandwiches around the pool at his apartment complex. At 9, he asked for an ice cream maker.

Cooking — and cooking with an entrepreneurial bent — came naturally. "It was something I always did," he said. By age 15, English was working in a Mexican restaurant in Branford, Connecticut, "slinging out tacos." But he found the work intensely gratifying. "I love the energy of the restaurant business," he said. "I think that was the first thing I dialed into."

First he'd take a stab at college, spending a year at Guilford College in Greensboro, North Carolina, where "I realized that college wasn't for me," he said. "I needed more of a

vocational education." He was interested in art — primarily sculpting and painting. But his fascination with food would lead him to the Culinary Institute of America. Art to food wasn't much of a stretch; he sees parallels. As a chef, he said, "You're putting something out there for people to judge. You're taking that risk," much as an artist does. The main difference: "Our medium is food."

English said he sees parallels between chef and musician as well. A great dish is, after all, put together like a great composition. Cooking, he said, is "about a feeling, a rhythm." And "repetition — practice," English said. "And God-given ability. I think I was blessed with that. There's a feeling, an intangible thing. Somebody's really good at what they do, that's something they were put on this earth to do."

That, it seems, was clear during English's time at the institute, where he was a diligent student. He refers to the school as "an institution of food," and appreciated that level of concentration. "It's the type of place you can glide through if you want," English said. "I made sure I got my money's worth. I had a lot of energy and I was always ambitious." He also attracted more than his share of attention: "I got grabbed out early."

After graduating in 1982, he went to work at Le Cote Basque in New York, and then moved to Italy, where he further developed the rustic Mediterranean-influenced style that would serve him so well in the future. It was a style that reflected his Italian heritage and "an innate sensibility of how I was brought up. It was the one that came most naturally to me."

Olives feels as Mediterranean as its menu, all stucco and tile in mustard, browns, and terracotta, filled with accent pieces that look as though they came straight from a Tuscan street market. If the weather's fine, you can dine outside on the patio and feel as sun-kissed as an olive, while you watch and listen to the magic wrought by the Fountains of Bellagio. The sun-drenched mood continues on Olives' menu, which lists the likes of rosemary flatbread with fig balsamic jam, prosciutto, and Gorgonzola; wild boar pappardelle with cipollini onion agrodolce and a mustard drizzle; and a grilled veal T-bone with caramelized endive, pasticcio, and porcini salad. "Please order the falling cake with your entrée," the menu advises. Do it. Lunch and dinner. Olives, Bellagio, 3600 Las Vegas Blvd. South; 702-693-8181 or www. bellagio.com.

"I studied French cooking," English said. "I studied the classics. I studied haute cuisine." But country food, with its hearty flavors, was a more natural fit — and he's known for interpreting those traditions. "Some of that," he said, "I like to play with."

When English returned from Italy, it was to serve as executive chef at a northern-Italian restaurant in Cambridge, Massachusetts. The culinary world, he pointed out, has changed vastly since those days.

"It wasn't really a profession," English said. In the case of many of his brethren, "you were working in a steakhouse," as a "glorified cook. There were a few 'continental' restaurants, if you will."

Boston's also a little conservative, he said, which he views as an outgrowth of its English heritage. And that tendency could be a little frustrating for a chef on the cutting edge. If English offered wild-boar prosciutto, for example, "they're like, 'What's that?'" he said of his customers. "In 1985, when I came back from Italy, a bowl of risotto was a tough sell," he said.

But a culinary movement had begun to take shape on the West Coast during the early '70s, led by Alice Waters and Jeremiah Tower, founders of the California culinary movement. Whether it spread quickly eastward or whether True Believers were already at work on the East Coast is open to interpretation (and argument), but Americans' attitudes toward food and restaurants

were undergoing a sea change. And English would do his part to further the cause, opening Olives in a 50-seat storefront in Charlestown, Massachusetts, in 1989. People immediately felt the appeal of the earthy, rustic Mediterranean food. It didn't take long for the accolades to begin, though he didn't have a sense of his growing fame. "I was kind of just cooking away, doing my thing," he said.

In 1991, English was named the Rising Star Chef of the Year by the James Beard Foundation. He remembered the ceremony well. "The who's who was there," English said, among them Wolfgang Puck and Barbara Lazaroff, then Puck's wife and business partner. "It was amazing."

Other honors would follow. In 1994, the Beard foundation named him Best Chef: Northeast. He received the first Robert Mondavi Award for Culinary Excellence from the winemaking company, and in 2001 was named Restaurateur of the Year by Bon Appetit magazine.

Boston remains his base. "Olives Boston is the test kitchen for everything we do," he said. He didn't plan to stay in Boston — intended to stick there for a year or two before moving on, maybe back to New York — but that wasn't what life, and the jobs that are such a big part of life, presented. "Fifteen years later, I'm still in Boston," he said. And the city offers a comfort level. "I like the sort of European feel of it, the educational side," English said. "I like being around smart people."

More restaurants would follow, including Olives Las Vegas, which opened with Bellagio in 1998. Las Vegas was a natural choice, English said. "It seems to be the thing to do, doesn't it?"

And a good fit as well. "One of the things I started to realize after I opened my first restaurant is it really is all about entertainment at all levels," English said. "The restaurant business has become an entertainment business in so many ways. What better place to be in the entertainment business than Las Vegas? It is the entertainment capital of the world."

Like other chefs with restaurants in Las Vegas, English said he enjoys the varied clientele the city brings him. "This town is a riot," he said. "One week it's the rodeo. The next week, it's NASCAR. I also really love that Vegas gets all walks of life. Eating and drinking is truly the greatest democracy in the world — the greatest equalizer of all. I always want my restaurants to be approachable on all levels."

Like other celebrity chefs with Las Vegas restaurants, he's focusing on building a local clientele. "The city itself has changed. It's not just the Strip anymore. I've really prided myself on catering to the 702," referring to Las Vegas' area code.

Which of his restaurants seems to be the most low-maintenance? "There's no such thing as an easy restaurant to run," he said. "There's no such thing as an overnight success."

He's philosophical about what Todd English the Industry has brought him. "If I had only one restaurant now, I'd say no, I won't open another. At this point in my career, I think I'd say I want to do other things." Another reason he might have hesitated to expand, he said, was a tough year in the aftermath of 9/11.

But he doesn't have one restaurant; he has more than a dozen. "It's kind of like I've created this monster I have to feed now," he said. And feed it he will. English's latest projects are a restaurant on the Queen Mary II, one at the Swan and Dolphin complex at Walt Disney World in Florida, one in Tokyo, and one in Seattle. As for the possibility of a corporate buyout, he said, "I've been approached — although the right offer would intrigue me."

Though English is certainly in the ranks of the celebrity chefs, he's not the household name that some are, and that's fine with him. "Wolfgang (Puck) is his own industry," English said. "He's been doing it the longest." As for Emeril Lagasse, he said, "what he did is create his own style and persona. I think he's gotten the average American to not be afraid to get in the kitchen, and that's pretty cool. I decided to take another route — not that I don't want to move in that direction." He just doesn't want his message to get lost in the process.

"I want it to be as clear as I can make it," English said. "Everything I'm about at this point is to build toward that. I don't want to be overexposed. I want to keep up

the intrigue." That said, "You can't do it forever. It's demanding. It's high-energy. It's constantly changing. I think at some point I'll dial out. I think ultimately, I'd like to teach," maybe open his own school, which he said would be more focused than he thinks most cooking schools are today.

English said that through his restaurants, his mission is "always to tell a story. It's about the idea of cooking food from where olives grow." And while he's possessed of a rare intensity, he wants his restaurants, and especially his food, to be viewed in simple — albeit paradoxical — manner. "I like it to be serious, but I like it to be fun," English said. "I like it to be serious fun."

Todd English's

PERSONAL FAVORITES

Parmesan Pudding with Pea Sauce

Halibut with Artichoke Crust

Deep Dish Apricot Pie

Todd English's

Parmesan Pudding with Pea Sauce

For Pudding:
1 ½ tablespoons unsalted butter
3 tablespoons all-purpose flour
1 cup milk
2 cups cream
2 teaspoons kosher salt
1 cup grated Parmesan cheese
3 egg yolks
1 whole egg
Pea Sauce (recipe follows)
Pea shoots, for garnish (optional)

For Pea Sauce:
1 ½ cups fresh or defrosted frozen sweet peas
¾ cup chicken broth
3 tablespoons heavy cream
¼ teaspoon kosher salt
⅛ teaspoon black pepper

Preheat oven to 325° F. Spray a 3- by 6-inch loaf pan with vegetable spray (or use a thin layer of butter) and line with parchment paper.

To make roux: in a saucepot over medium heat, combine butter and flour and cook until a paste forms — about 5 minutes. Be careful not to brown.

Combine milk and cream. While roux is still on the burner, slowly whisk in milk mixture to roux. Whisk well to combine. Bring to a boil, still whisking.

Add salt and Parmesan cheese. Return to a boil.

In a large bowl, combine egg yolks and whole egg.

Be sure to break the yolks and combine well.

Remove pan from the heat and whisk milk mixture into the egg mixture.

Strain entire mixture through a chinoise or other fine sieve and pour into lined pan.

Cover with foil and place in larger pan; fill with water to come halfway up loaf pan. Bake for 1 ½ to 2 hours, being careful that liquid does not touch the top of the pan. It will still jiggle in the middle and the edges may be slightly rounded, but not souffled. Remove from water bath and cool to room temperature. Then refrigerate overnight — very important.

To serve: unmold the pudding onto a cutting board. Cut into 6 to 8 slices and place each slice in the center of a heatproof plate. Place plates in the oven at 325° F and heat until the pudding is just warm, about 2 to 3 minutes.

For the Pea Sauce: Place the peas, chicken broth, cream, salt, and pepper in a blender and blend until smooth. Place in a small saucepan over very low heat and cook until warm, about 2 minutes.

Pour the sauce around the pudding slices and garnish with the pea shoots.

Serves 6 to 8.

Todd English's

Halibut with Artichoke Crust

Artichoke crust:
6 fresh, frozen or canned artichoke bottoms
1 teaspoon fresh thyme leaves
3 garlic cloves
¼ cup nonfat buttermilk or yogurt
1 tablespoon Dijon mustard
2 tablespoons plain bread crumbs
¼ teaspoon kosher salt
¼ teaspoon black pepper

Halibut:
4 6-ounce halibut fillets
½ teaspoon kosher salt
¼ teaspoon black pepper
12 baby artichokes, thinly sliced through the heart,
or 2 tablespoons bread crumbs

To make the artichoke crust: place the artichoke bottoms, thyme, garlic, buttermilk or yogurt, mustard, bread crumbs, salt, and pepper in a food processor fitted with a steel blade and process until smooth.

For halibut: Sprinkle the halibut with salt and pepper. Divide the artichoke crust into 4 portions and place dollops on the top side (non-skin side) only of the halibut fillets. Pat down to form a crust.

Cover the artichoke crust with the artichoke slices or sprinkle with bread crumbs.

Place a large nonstick skillet over medium-high heat and when it is hot, add the halibut fillets, skin-side down. Cook until the skin is crispy, about 2 minutes. Transfer to the oven and bake until the halibut is rare, about 10 minutes.

Serve immediately.

Serves 4.

Todd English's

Deep Dish Apricot Pie

Topping and crust:
3 sticks unsalted butter
¾ cup sugar
1 cup steel-cut oats
1 cup stone-ground yellow cornmeal
1 cup flour
1 teaspoon ground ginger
1 teaspoon ground allspice

Filling:
1 cup (packed) golden brown sugar
2 large eggs
1 teaspoon vanilla extract
¼ cup heavy cream
3 tablespoons unsalted butter, melted
1 teaspoon ground allspice
1 teaspoon ground ginger
¼ teaspoon salt
1 ½ cups coarsely chopped walnuts
1 ½ cups dried apricots (about 8 ounces),
cut into ½-inch pieces
1 cup fresh apricots, peeled and pitted,
sliced into quarters
Additional dried apricots and
walnuts, for garnish

To make topping and crust: Using a hand or stand mixer, cream the butter. Mix in the sugar. Add the oats, cornmeal, flour, and spices. Press half of mixture into a deep dish 9-inch pie plate to form crust.

Preheat oven to 375° F.

To make filling: whisk brown sugar, eggs, and vanilla extract in large bowl to blend. Whisk in cream, melted butter, spices, and salt. Stir in chopped walnuts and apricots.

Transfer filling to prepared crust. Sprinkle with remaining topping mixture. Bake until filling is set and crust is golden, tenting pie with foil if crust browns too quickly, about 1 hour. Transfer pie to rack; cool pie completely. (Can be prepared 1 day ahead. Cover pie and store at room temperature.)

Garnish pie with additional dried apricots and walnuts. Serve pie at room temperature.

Serves 8.

Cindy Hutson

Ortanique

"I've done so many other things. This is definitely my calling."

Caribbean cookery may seem like a stretch for a girl from New Jersey, but Cindy Hutson earned her tropical chops.

There were the inevitable detours. She graduated early from high school in Berkeley Heights, New Jersey, and went to work at a home for disabled children. She loved the work. "That was the most rewarding time of my life," Hutson said. "Those kids grounded me."

But after two years, it seemed time to move on. "My parents had great hopes for me to go to nursing school," she said. Hutson had other ideas: "I packed up my car and headed to Florida. I said, 'I'm going to fish.'"

She'd long been an avid fisherman. Her father loved the sport and his eldest son had a tendency toward abject seasickness, so it was daughter Cindy who got to go out in the boat for bluefish, flounder, shark, and crab. She learned how to clean it, how to cook it properly.

Her interest in cooking started early as well. Hutson was, at age 9, a fan of TV's *Galloping Gourmet* Graham Kerr. "I'd come home from school and watch that religiously," Hutson said. "All of my friends would be playing kickball in the street. I thought what a beautiful thing, to create food like that. And he always had a glass of wine" — the ultimate in '60s chic.

Cindy Hutson's Ortanique is, you might say, a little like the island region it reflects: It's a little out of the way, a little hard to find, tucked into a walkway that connects Paris and Bally's. It looks a little exotic to visitors who walk by and see the candlelamps burning inside, but once they're in, they find a place that's both elegant and comfortable. Lights are soft but accents loom large, as in the big-screen underwater scene that drifts across one end of the restaurant, lending a Zenlike quality. Keep your eyes peeled and you might see the bandanna-wearing Hutson, who pops in about once a month from her other restaurants in Miami and Washington, D.C., to prepare her "cuisine of the sun," in her own version of island-hopping. To experience it, start with West Indian curried crab cakes or duck confit spring rolls and move on to pan-sautéed Florida black grouper, Caribbean bouillabaisse, or a jerked double pork chop. Dinner only. Ortanique, Paris Las Vegas, 3655 Las Vegas Blvd. South; 702-946-4346 or www.caesars.com.

She also was learning to appreciate fresh produce. While most of America tends to think of New Jersey as an urban renewal project waiting to happen, Hutson noted that it is, after all, the Garden State, with agricultural resources that were even more abundant when she was a child. On Sunday mornings, she remembers, "we'd all hop in the car" for jaunts to apple orchards, cornfields, and more.

But it was fishing that was closest to Hutson's heart. After she moved to Miami in 1978, she took a boating course. She and her boyfriend, then husband, now ex-husband, bought a boat and ran charters out of Islamorada to places like Bimini, the Bahamas, and Mexico.

"We just took people wherever they wanted to go," she said. "I spent five years doing nothing but fishing." Well, she did a little more than fish; Hutson had her first child during that time. "I fished pregnant up until the point where I couldn't gaff fish anymore," she said.

She was, a little improbably, learning a little about the restaurant business, too. Most of the boat's passengers were northern tourists who didn't want — or just couldn't manage to take home — the tuna, wahoo, and other fish they caught. Hutson would clean it and sell it to local restaurants. "At that point, you'd have never convinced me I'd be doing what I am now," she said.

The marriage fell apart, and along with it the business. Hutson, a single mother, had to find a new job. In what would be the only time she'd work in someone else's restaurant, she became a waitress. At Miami's Doral Country Club. During the height of the winter season.

"I was the worst waitress, but I probably made more money than anybody, because I was so friendly," Hutson said. "The people felt sorry for me. And whenever anybody got mad at me, I'd joke around with them until it was all right."

She started dating the Jamaican man who would become her second husband. Knowing of her fondness for Jamaican Blue Mountain coffee, he'd have his mother bring a supply on her frequent trips from Jamaica. And then one day the woman's husband asked Hutson if she thought there was a market for the coffee in the United States. She was confident there was. He agreed to back a venture, and Hutson was in business again. And the new partners jumped in with both feet.

"Without a client base, we brought in a containerload," which Hutson estimated at about 3,000 pounds. "Which leads us to our first mistake," she said. "Coffee's perishable." They took out an ad in *Gourmet* magazine. Response was strong, but they still sold only about half of the load. "Thank God it wasn't my money," Hutson said.

It was a hard lesson learned, but the business did take off. She started traveling to trade shows. "People fell in love with the coffee," she said. "We built up our client base and sold it across the United States — including to Starbucks, when they only had a few stores."

Then Hurricane Gilbert hit Jamaica, in 1988. The coffee crop was devastated. And Jamaican Blue Mountain coffee plants take six years to

bear fruit. "I realized I had all my eggs in one basket," Hutson said. "What do I do now?"

Jamaican condiments and jerk spices and sauces would be the answer. Hutson began representing the Busha Browne's Company Ltd., a Jamaican manufacturer. She was still going to trade shows, still selling a food product, but "instead of my coffee, I had to cook for all these people."

She discovered that she liked the creativity the job engendered, and also the fact that the food she was creating "was healthy and very, very flavorful." She traveled from island to island — Barbados, Martinique, all over the Bahamas — and learned a little more on each trip. She combined and adapted, and impressed Caribbean natives with her versions of traditional foods.

Hutson would still sell the coffee (and, because of her reputation for integrity, would become the first person the Jamaican Coffee Board allowed to take green beans out of the country), but the condiment line would be her mainstay.

She had two more children. And then, in 1994, she and her husband separated. She was out of business yet again. "It was a family business," Hutson said. "It got real sticky."

By that time she'd met Norma Shirley, a restaurateur known as the Julia Child of the Caribbean. While Hutson was still doing trade shows, a man stopped by her booth one day. He's been sent by his mother, Norma

Shirley. Delius Shirley started calling Hutson to obtain products his mother used in her restaurant but couldn't get in Jamaica. He'd come to Miami to pick up the products, and he and Hutson would get together.

"We developed a relationship out of love of fine food," she said. He became, she said, "my partner in business and in life."

Delius Shirley wanted to leave Jamaica. "Miami," Hutson said, "was getting really hot." He convinced her they should open a restaurant. They found a little spot on Lincoln Road on Miami's pre-trendy South Beach. "I had a feeling about Lincoln Road, that it was going to come back," she said.

They scrounged up the money, re-doing the restaurant themselves with the help of a contractor friend. Finally, it was ready. "I said, 'Who are we hiring to be the chef?'" Hutson remembered.

Shirley's reply: "You are going to be the chef."

"Do you want to lose every penny?" she asked. "I had assumed he was going to ask his mother to be the chef. So I wrote a menu," she said. "It was all Jamaican stuff."

They called it Norma's on the Beach, because they couldn't afford a public-relations agency and decided to capitalize on Norma Shirley's name. Norma told her, "If you screw up my name, I'll kill you."

"She scared me into doing the right thing," Hutson said. They opened right

ORTANIQUE
Cuisine of The Sun

after Thanksgiving 1994. Delius Shirley ran the front of the house, Hutson the back — which consisted of her, a prepper and a dishwasher. She didn't know much about restaurant kitchens. She wore "a little sundress and a little apron" instead of chef's whites. She was burning herself, cutting herself. "Needless to say, I cried for three months straight," Hutson said. "I didn't understand how hard it could be."

Then *USA Today* discovered Norma's, mentioning it in a story on the revival of South Beach. Other articles, and plaudits, followed. But all of the attention led to mixed feelings for Hutson, because "everybody thought Norma was in the kitchen. I was working 16, 17 hours a day in tears, and my name wasn't even being put in the paper."

Eventually, the news spread, "because there was nothing like it anywhere," she said. And as one of the few female chefs in Miami — which she said isn't the case anymore — she also was earning the respect of her peers. Norman Van Aken, dean of Miami's culinary cutting edge, sent CNN to Hutson's door.

Then Robert Johnson saw an article about Hutson in *Ocean Drive* magazine. At the time, Johnson owned Black Entertainment Television, and he was thinking of opening a few restaurants. He was intrigued.

Johnson came to the restaurant late one evening. Hutson, in the kitchen all day, was sweaty and tired. Shirley told her she needed to come out and talk to a man

at a table. She refused. He prodded. She refused again. He prodded some more. She relented. Johnson told her he was interested in hiring her to do some consulting work. He'd be back in town in a couple of weeks.

It was a few weeks before Mother's Day, which was to be Hutson's first day off in more than 18 months. Shirley had given the kids money to take her out and was going to fill in in the kitchen. Johnson proposed that they meet on Mother's Day.

"No, I'm not," Hutson remembered saying. "I'm not going to meet with him on Mother's Day." Then the kids found out who Johnson was. "BET?" they said. "Oh, my God, Mom. That's awesome!"

The kids took a rain check. Hutson met with Johnson and agreed to act as a consultant for restaurants at Walt Disney World in Washington, D.C. "Then he got the option to take this space," she said, sitting inside Ortanique at Paris Hotel-Casino in Las Vegas.

And then Hutson and Shirley found a site in Coral Gables that would be perfect for a new restaurant. Johnson agreed to back them. It opened in July 1999, and this time, Norma's name would not be involved; instead the restaurant was named for the ortanique, a citrus fruit native to Jamaica that Hutson said is a sweet cross between a tangerine, an orange, and a unique fruit, the latter akin to a grapefruit. In the new location, she could depart from purely Caribbean fare. They'd

planned to keep Norma's on the Beach, "but my heart and soul were not in it," Hutson said.

Then BET was purchased by Viacom, which had no interest in BET's restaurants. Johnson offered the Las Vegas and Washington, D.C., locations to Hutson and Shirley. The Las Vegas Ortanique opened in 2001 — three days before 9/11. "It was very difficult," Hutson said. "We basically just ran a ghost crew to keep the quality of the food for the small amount of diners we had." Today, she said, she and Shirley split their time between the three locations, spending about 10 days a month in each, their time overlapping whenever possible.

But while she's gradually becoming a restaurant mogul, she said her gratification doesn't come from making money, beyond having enough "to put my kids through college." What is important is providing comfort for her customers. "Especially now, with the war and 9/11 and anthrax and all the other things our world has brought to us, what I want to do is be a place of contentment for people," she said. "If I can accomplish that, I've accomplished what I want to do."

And the child-care worker turned fisherwoman turned waitress turned chef has finally found a comfort zone for herself. "I've done so many other things," Hutson said. "This is definitely my calling."

Cindy Hutson's

PERSONAL FAVORITES

Crab Cakes

Marinated Grouper

Strawberry Wonton Napoleons

Cindy Hutson's

Crab Cakes

2 eggs
2 tablespoons curry powder
1 teaspoon kosher salt
¾ cup scallions, trimmed, washed, and
finely chopped
1 red pepper
1 yellow pepper
1 small red onion
1 bunch parsley
2 pounds jumbo lump crabmeat
(pick out shell fragments)
1 tablespoon Worcestershire sauce
¼ cup high-quality mayonnaise
¼ cup whole-grain mustard
2 cups panko bread crumbs (Japanese bread
crumbs, available at Asian markets and
some supermarkets)
Clarified butter or canola oil

Beat eggs in a stainless steel bowl. Add curry powder and salt. Set aside for the curry to bloom.

Meanwhile, place chopped scallions in another bowl. Remove seeds and stems from peppers and dice small. Add the diced peppers to the scallion bowl. Peel and cut red onion in small dice and add to peppers and scallions. Wash and pick over parsley, discarding stems. Chop finely and add to scallion mixture.

Gently pick through crabmeat and remove any cartilage. Set aside.

Whisk the Worcestershire, mayonnaise, and mustard into the egg and curry. Add all of the vegetables and toss until well mixed. Gently add the crabmeat, folding into the curry mixture and trying not to break apart the crabmeat. Then fold in enough panko bread crumbs to hold the crab mixture together. Form into patties.

Using a little clarified butter or canola oil, brown crab cakes on each side, then finish cooking for 8 to 10 minutes in a 400° F oven.

Serves 6.

Marinated Grouper

6 8-ounce grouper fillets
1 tablespoon lemon-pepper seasoning
¼ cup sesame oil
¼ cup teriyaki sauce
2 garlic cloves, chopped
4 tablespoons salted butter
Hot cooked jasmine rice
Grouper Sauce (recipe follows)
Parsley leaves for garnish

For Grouper Sauce:
4 tablespoons salted butter
2 large Vidalia onions, peeled and thinly sliced
1 cup Bacardi Limon
1 12-ounce jar pepper jelly (preferably
Busha Browne's)
2 cups water
¾ cup teriyaki sauce

Have your fishmonger cut the grouper into 7- to 8-ounce portions, leaving out the bloodline of the fish. Sprinkle the fillets with lemon-pepper seasoning. Place the sesame oil, teriyaki sauce, and garlic in a stainless steel bowl and whisk together with a fork. Add the fish, making sure the marinade coats the fish. Set aside in the refrigerator for at least 2 hours.

Cooking the grouper: Preheat oven to 400° F. Using a large skillet, place butter on medium-high heat. After the pan has heated and butter melts, add the grouper pieces. Brown in the butter for about 4 to 5 minutes and then flip. Brown on the other side for about 2 minutes and then finish cooking the fish in the preheated oven, about 8 minutes (make sure the sauté pan has an ovenproof handle).

Grouper Sauce: In a medium-sized saucepan, melt the butter on medium-high heat. Add the onions, turn the heat down to medium and caramelize slowly. Stir occasionally so the onions do not burn. Once the onions have gotten soft and are golden brown, deglaze the pan by pouring in the Bacardi Limon. Stir in the pepper jelly and add the water. Simmer for about 5 to 10 minutes and then add the teriyaki sauce. Remove from heat.

Pour the sauce into a blender. Cover the top of the blender with a kitchen towel and pulse the blender to let some heat escape. Then blend smooth for about 3 to 5 minutes. Set aside for saucing the grouper.

To serve: Warm 6 large plates and place the jasmine rice in the center. Carefully place the cooked fish on top of the rice and spoon the heated sauce on top of the fish. Garnish with parsley leaves and serve with sautéed haricot verts or other green vegetables.

Serves 6.

Cindy Hutson's

Strawberry Wonton Napoleons

2 pints fresh strawberries
1 cup granulated sugar (or more or less, to taste)
1 tablespoon red food coloring
2 teaspoons balsamic vinegar
4 large fresh basil leaves
18 wonton skins
Oil for frying
Granulated sugar
2 cups cream, whipped and sweetened to taste

Wash, dry and quarter the strawberries and place in a small mixing bowl. Sprinkle granulated sugar over the berries and pour food coloring and balsamic vinegar over the berries.

Chiffonade (thinly slice) basil leaves and mix into strawberry-sugar mix.

Allow to chill for approximately 30 minutes in order to allow the sugar to melt and form a syrup and also to allow the basil to perfume the syrup.

Fry wontons individually and toss while hot in granulated sugar. Set aside.

To serve: Each Napoleon will use three fried and sugared wontons with some of the strawberry mix and whipped cream. Stack alternating ingredients, placing a wonton down and then adding strawberry mix, followed by whipped cream and then another stack. Top off with whipped cream. Pour excess strawberry-balsamic-basil syrup around the base of the plate for decoration.

Serves 6.

Julian Serrano

Picasso

"I want to tell people they are coming to some place very consistent. Simple, elegant flavors. The food is not confused, not trying to do too many things."

Some chefs find their life's path through the kitchen because of a fascination with food that borders on a religious calling. Julian Serrano's was dictated by a finely honed sense of pragmatism.

"At a very young age, I wanted to travel," said Serrano, a native of Madrid. "I had an independent streak, and I wanted to travel outside Spain." The kitchen, he decided, could be a means to that end. "If I knew how to cook, I could go anyplace and I could work." So at 16, he entered a six-month culinary program in Marbella. And as it turned out, he was a natural. "I was very good," Serrano said. "It was easy for me to do it."

He'd need that natural talent to get through his first job. At 17, Serrano went to work for a very exacting Belgian who had a French restaurant outside Marbella. "I had to portion the meat and clean it when each order came in," instead of portioning it in advance, he said. "I never understood it, but that was the way he liked it."

The portions had to be perfect — the owner would weigh them to be sure. "He was crazy," Serrano said. "He was also a very good cook." Frustrating though it may have been at the time ("I used to go to my room crazy — so much pressure"), it would leave Serrano with a well-developed discipline.

His next jobs would be easy by comparison. Serrano moved on to a hotel in the same area, where he stayed for a couple of years, and then began his compulsory military service of 13 months. In the military, he cooked for 300 officers — and learned about business in the process. "It was great experience because we had to go to the market every day; there was no call to the purveyor," he said. "And we had a budget."

Service commitment fulfilled, Serrano began traveling in earnest. He went first to the Cayman Islands to work in a hotel, staying there for about three years. Then he moved to Miami and jobs with the Carnival and Emerald Sea cruise lines, which were in their fledgling years in the 70s. Carnival was making one- and two-week cruises, but Serrano preferred the Emerald Sea's day trips to the Bahamas. Seems like an odd choice, but again, the pragmatist: "A lot of times you get to go to different places, but you're not seeing the place, because you're working."

Serrano was getting valuable experience, feeding 1,000 people in three hours at both lunch and dinner. But after two and a half years, he had wearied of both ships and Miami. "If I stayed in Miami, I'd only speak Spanish," he said. "I wanted to learn the language." Besides, "I had a different picture of America than Miami."

It doesn't get much different than Nashville, and that was Serrano's next stop. Vizcaya was "the only Spanish restaurant I ever worked in in my life," Serrano said — and that includes his work in Spain.

Nashville posed challenges aplenty. "It wasn't easy in the restaurant business 20, 30 years

Picasso the man was generally a restless soul, but Picasso the restaurant is a serene spot away from the often frenetic pace of the Bellagio. Seek out the escalator tucked between the Rodeo Drive-level shops in the Via Bellagio shopping area and take it down to lakeside and the big wooden doors that provide a portal to Picasso. Those doors will be the only intimidating thing you'll encounter, as the restaurant is as colorful and progressive as the man and his art. The ceiling is high, coved and warm with the richness of wood, the floor a crazy-quilt carpet of color. Yes, those are genuine Picasso paintings and sculptures, and there's art beyond the windows, too, in the form of the Fountains of Bellagio. Julian Serrano continually changes his listings in the four-course Tasting Menu and five-course Chef's Degustation to bring his customers the best of the season, but among his classics are a boudin of fresh lobster, shrimp, and scallops, and sautéed medallions of fallow deer with caramelized green apples and Zinfandel sauce. Dinner only. Picasso, Bellagio, 3600 Las Vegas Blvd. South; 702-693-7223 or www. bellagio.com.

ago," Serrano said. "There was no fresh fish. The people in general didn't like to try new things. It was not easy for a young chef." But this young chef had already decided to stay in his new country, so while in Nashville, he applied for a green card. And then, a career-making opportunity arose: A Nashville acquaintance moved on to Maisonette in Cincinnati, one of the most highly regarded restaurants in the country. Introductions were made, and another Belgian chef offered Serrano a job.

One little problem: His green-card application was making its way through the system, and Serrano didn't want to risk any snags by changing location. That card was more important to him than Maisonette.

There would be other opportunities. Serrano got a call from Tampa's Columbia Restaurant, which has been serving Cuban and Spanish food for nearly 100 years. He went for the interview and discovered a behemoth of a place that seats more than 1,600. "I saw the restaurant and I thought, 'I'm not ready for this,'" he said.

Then another friend left for San Francisco. "Right away, he put San Francisco in my

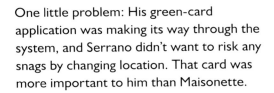

mind." Green card in hand, he decided to leave for the coast. "Everything I owned fit in my car," Serrano said. He was 26 or 27. He bumped around San Francisco for a while, working in a Mexican restaurant, a top-rated German restaurant (where he met his future wife, Susan), and then Sutter 500, where he worked for a year and a half with Michelin three-star chef Roger Verge.

And then, an experience that would leave perhaps the biggest mark on Serrano's professional life: A chef at Sutter 500 told him he was not sufficiently dedicated — that he liked tennis and fun too much to be a serious chef. "You have to focus on something," he

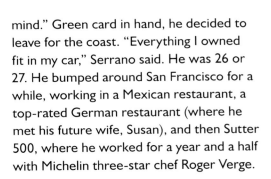

♠

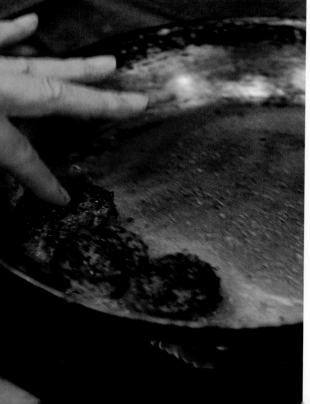

told Serrano. "If it's cooking, focus on cooking 100 percent." The criticism hit home. When Serrano moved on to the Poissonier, for which Verge was a consultant, he rededicated himself to the art and craft of cooking.

Not long after, he discovered that the owner of the acclaimed Masa's, Masataka Kobayashi, was giving a demonstration at Macy's. Serrano went to see him, and Masa invited him to come by the restaurant. After they talked, Masa said he didn't have any positions, but would call when he did. A week later, in February 1984, he offered Serrano a job as sous chef. At Masa's, Serrano only strengthened his dedication — "I think because of him and the food he was doing," he said. "I lost a few friends because I was talking about food all the time."

But soon, he'd lose his new mentor. Masa was murdered November 19, 1984. The maitre d' found the chef dead in his apartment, but kept the news from the staff until the following evening so business would go on as usual. When Serrano went home that night, his wife had seen a report of Masa's death on the news.

Co-owner Bill Kimpton had decided to keep the restaurant open, but seven months later, Serrano and his wife took off for Europe,

where he would further hone his skills, working in Switzerland and France. When she got pregnant, they decided to return to the United States. He got a call from Masa's but didn't want to return. He worked in New York, but wasn't really comfortable there. Soon San Francisco called again; the chef at Masa's wanted to give Serrano his job.

"I said, 'Not yet,'" Serrano remembered. But the chef was too stressed. He told Kimpton he wanted Serrano to take over. Serrano refused, but suggested the chef take two weeks off to rest. And rest he did: "He didn't come back." And so at age 32, in 1985, Serrano was running his own restaurant.

"I told Bill I'd work hard and do the best I can," he said. He was working 17 hours a day, and planned to stay only two years. He stayed for 16 years, racking up honors along the way. Then, as is the case of so many celebrity chefs who land in Las Vegas, gaming mogul Steve Wynn came calling. Actually, it was Mirage executive Gamal Aziz who called. Aziz had offered Serrano a job at Caesars eight years before. "I came to Vegas. I said no," he said with a grimace. This time, Aziz offered Serrano a Spanish restaurant, the theme inspired by the Picasso paintings on the walls. "I'm not interested in a Spanish restaurant," he replied.

Wynn kept calling, and eventually agreed on a French-Mediterranean theme. But Serrano's daughter, Estefania, was in a good school in San Francisco, and Susan Serrano had been diagnosed with a brain tumor and was undergoing medical care, which ultimately proved successful. "Vegas, when you don't know, you think it's the end of the world," Serrano said.

Then Susan Serrano told her husband she thought Las Vegas would be more international than San Francisco. "I looked at her and said, 'You're crazy,'" he said.

Wynn pressed for a decision. Serrano was plagued with thoughts of a life-changing opportunity that his gardener father had let pass. "Obviously, the answer was yes," he said. "Sometimes, you have to make a decision." And he knew he could always return to San Francisco if things went south.

Serrano remembered being depressed in the beginning. The family moved to Las Vegas during the dog days of August and lived in the Mirage for the first two months. It might be a glamorous resort to those who visit, but living there was wearing thin. He soon realized the move had been a good decision, and establishing his own home helped. "For me, Las Vegas is perfect," he said. "I like it every day more."

The acclaim for Picasso was instant. "The timing was right," Serrano said. "Vegas was ready for that. The people were ready for that. Everything was perfect." He was so

happy, in fact, that although his contract gave him an out if Wynn were to sell the Bellagio, when the sale did come in 2000, he decided to stay on with the new MGM-Mirage.

And while he continually strives to make Picasso better, he knows that day-to-day reliability is most important. "I want to tell people they are coming to some place very consistent," Serrano said. "Simple, elegant flavors. The food is not confused, not trying to do too many things."

Serrano has long been a big believer in charitable work, contributing dinners for charity auctions and taking part in various fund-raisers across the country. "I always do it because I think I'm very lucky to be in the position I am," he said. "I like to help people."

And while some celebrity chefs manage from afar, Serrano says he thinks it's important that he maintain his presence at Picasso. "We taste — the cook, myself, the sommelier ," he said. "Did we make the right decision? It's important to be here, and to offer the customer a good experience."

♠

Julian Serrano's

PERSONAL FAVORITES

Lobster with Caramelized Carrots

Potato Pancakes with Crème Fraiche & Osetra Caviar

Roasted Breast of Pheasant
with Pears, Morels & Wild Rice Risotto

Julian Serrano's

Lobster with Caramelized Carrots

For Sauce:
2 lobster carcasses
2 tablespoons extra-virgin olive oil
½ cup brandy
1 cup mirepoix (see note)
1 tablespoon tomato paste
4 cups water
1 sprig tarragon
½ cup crème fraiche
2 tablespoons unsalted butter
Salt
Pepper

For Carrot Garnish:
9 ⅛-inch-thick slices of carrot
cut on the bias
2 tablespoons unsalted butter
Pinch of powdered sugar
1 whole carrot
1 cup grapeseed oil

For Lobster:
1 1-pound lobster
½ teaspoon lobster caviar

To prepare the sauce: crush the carcasses in a large bowl. Heat the olive oil in a large sauté pan and sauté the pieces of carcass for 5 minutes, until they begin to brown. Add the brandy, mirepoix, tomato paste, water, and tarragon and cook for 25 to 30 minutes. Pass the liquid through a fine sieve and reduce to approximately 1 ½ cups. Add the crème fraiche and the butter. Salt and pepper to taste.

For the caramelized carrots: boil the bias-cut pieces of carrot in salted water until al dente. Drain. Heat the butter in a sauté pan and add the cooked carrots. Sprinkle with powdered sugar and sauté for 1 minute, until they become golden in color.

To make the carrot confit: peel the whole carrot. Using a mandoline or slicing machine, slice the

carrot paper-thin, lengthwise. Trim the slices to a uniform 4 inches in length and make a very fine julienne using a very sharp knife. Bring the grapeseed oil up to medium heat in a deep sauté pan. Add the carrot julienne and cook until tender.

Remove the carrots from the oil and raise the heat to medium-high. Return the carrots to the oil for 15 seconds. Remove and drain on a towel.

To finish the dish: cook the lobster in boiling water for 4 minutes. Remove from the water and separate the meat from the shell, being careful not to break the tail. Cut the tail in half lengthwise. Arrange the caramelized carrot slices in the shape of a flower in the center of the serving plate. Place half of the tail meat on either side of the flower

and set the claws on the top and bottom of the tail pieces. Lightly spoon the sauce over the lobster meat and place the carrot confit on top. Sprinkle the dish with lobster caviar.

Serves 1.

NOTE: Mirepoix is a mixture of diced vegetables — usually onions, carrots, and celery — and herbs sautéed in butter. It is used to season various dishes, including sauces and soups. A common ratio is 5 ounces carrots to 4 ounces onions and 2 ounces celery, seasoned with a sprig of thyme and ½ bay leaf.

Julian Serrano's

Potato Pancakes with
Crème Fraiche & Osetra Caviar

1 large potato
½ medium onion, finely chopped
1 egg
2 teaspoons flour
¾ cup vegetable oil
Osetra caviar, to taste
2 tablespoons crème fraiche

For potato pancakes: Peel and finely grate the
potato. Add chopped onion, egg, and flour; mix
thoroughly. Put the oil in a medium-sized sauté pan
and bring to medium-high heat. Place teaspoon-
sized dollops of the potato mixture in the sauté pan
and cook for about 2 minutes on each side, until
they are crispy golden brown.

To serve: place pancakes on the serving plates
and place a dollop of caviar on top of each of the
pancakes. Drizzle the plate with the crème fraiche.

Serves 2.

Julian Serrano's

Roasted Breast of Pheasant with Pears, Morels, & Wild Rice Risotto

For Risotto:
1 cup wild rice
3 cups chicken stock
1 cup water
1 tablespoon chopped carrots
1 tablespoon chopped onion
1 tablespoon chopped celery
¼ cup roasted pine nuts
2 shiitake mushrooms, chopped
1 tablespoon butter
¼ cup Parmesan cheese
Salt
Pepper

For Pear:
½ pear
½ cup pear liqueur
½ cup white wine

For Pheasant:
1 pheasant
2 tablespoons extra-virgin olive oil
½ cup white wine
½ cup chicken stock
Mirepoix (see note)
1 clove garlic
1 tablespoon tomato paste
Bay leaves
White peppercorns

Water
1 shallot
½ cup Port
¼ cup red wine
10 morels (dried preferred)
2 baby carrots, cooked
4 asparagus spears, cooked

For Rice: Rinse the rice. Put the rice in a large stockpot with the stock and water. Cook until it boils and place in a hot oven (about 450° F) for at least 20 minutes. When the rice is almost done, add the vegetables, pine nuts, and, in the last minute, the chopped shiitake. When all of the liquid is gone, add butter and Parmesan. Mix together; salt and pepper to taste. Put into a lightly greased cup to form into 2 timbales.

For Pear: Peel the pear. Clean and slice the pear width-wise into ¼-inch slices. Add pear liqueur and white wine and cook in a double boiler until pear is tender.

For Pheasant: Separate legs from breast and reserve legs for the sauce. Salt and pepper the breast. Heat oil (medium-high to high heat) in sauté pan and sauté breast until golden brown. Place in a hot oven (500° F.) for 5 minutes. Remove from oven and allow to rest.

Retain bones from pheasant and sauté in olive oil until the bones are crispy and have a good dark color. Then deglaze pan with white wine. Add chicken stock, mirepoix, garlic, tomato paste, bay leaves, white peppercorns, and water to cover the bones and cook over slow heat for 30 minutes. Then strain and reserve liquid.

Put diced shallot, Port and red wine in a saucepan over medium-high heat. Reduce until almost all of the Port is gone. Add reserved liquid, salt and pepper to taste and cook for 30 minutes.

To serve: After cooking, bone the breast. Slice the breast in 4 pieces. In between each slice of pheasant, put 1 slice of pear, and fan the medallions along the bottom half of the plate. Then nap the pheasant and the pears with the pheasant sauce and place a morel at each slice of the breast. Place the contents of 1 rice timbale in the center of the top half of the plate. On either side of the rice, place 1 baby carrot and 2 asparagus spears.

Serves 2.

NOTE: Mirepoix is a mixture of diced vegetables — usually onions, carrots, and celery — and herbs sautéed in butter. It is used to seasons various dishes, including sauces and soups. A common ratio is 5 ounces carrots to 4 ounces onions and 2 ounces celery, seasoned with a sprig of thyme and ½ bay leaf.

Wolfgang Puck

Postrio

"At the end of the day, for me the most important thing is that the customers are happy, and that they come back."

As the twenty-first century gets its legs, Las Vegas is known as a fine dining mecca — one of the best restaurant cities in the country, maybe even in the world. But that wasn't the case when Wolfgang Puck came to town. Until the early '90s, Las Vegas was known for its bargain buffets and big cheap slabs of prime rib — and not much else, at least as far as restaurants were concerned.

Still, Puck decided to join the long line of entrepreneurs who decided, for better or worse, to gamble on Sin City. Retail developers Sheldon Gordon and Mel Simon, friends of Puck, were building the Forum Shops at Caesars. "Sheldon was looking for tenants," Puck said.

Puck was no stranger to Las Vegas. "I always used to go to watch the fights. I said, 'Why not go there and do a restaurant?'" His eyes were open: "I thought it was a risk, in a way."

But he had yet to find out just how much of a risk. Spago Las Vegas opened in early December 1992. And those who know Las Vegas know just how quiet things are during most of December. "In the first few weeks of December, it was so slow, I thought I was going to kill myself," Puck said. "The way Sheldon was telling me, it would be 24 hours a day and crazy. The first time we opened, I said, 'Jesus Christ, there are only 40 dinners, and the next day only 60 dinners.' And it continued like that."

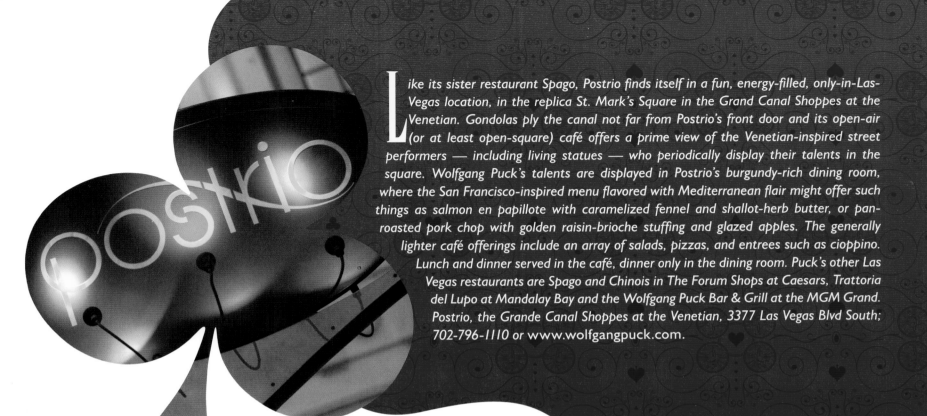

Postrio

Like its sister restaurant Spago, Postrio finds itself in a fun, energy-filled, only-in-Las-Vegas location, in the replica St. Mark's Square in the Grand Canal Shoppes at the Venetian. Gondolas ply the canal not far from Postrio's front door and its open-air (or at least open-square) café offers a prime view of the Venetian-inspired street performers — including living statues — who periodically display their talents in the square. Wolfgang Puck's talents are displayed in Postrio's burgundy-rich dining room, where the San Francisco-inspired menu flavored with Mediterranean flair might offer such things as salmon en papillote with caramelized fennel and shallot-herb butter, or pan-roasted pork chop with golden raisin-brioche stuffing and glazed apples. The generally lighter café offerings include an array of salads, pizzas, and entrees such as cioppino. Lunch and dinner served in the café, dinner only in the dining room. Puck's other Las Vegas restaurants are Spago and Chinois in The Forum Shops at Caesars, Trattoria del Lupo at Mandalay Bay and the Wolfgang Puck Bar & Grill at the MGM Grand. Postrio, the Grande Canal Shoppes at the Venetian, 3377 Las Vegas Blvd South; 702-796-1110 or www.wolfgangpuck.com.

Things would pick up in a few days, people around him promised: the National Finals Rodeo — always a bright spot of busy-ness during the quiet of December — was on the way. But that would provide a little bit of culture shock for Puck. He started noticing all the cowboy hats, all the tight jeans and pointed boots and big belt buckles. He thought these locals dressed a little differently than the people back home in California.

"I thought they were people from Vegas," Puck said. Only later did he find out that many NFR fans come from "Oklahoma or east Texas or somewhere." But if the NFR fans seemed a little strange to Puck, they apparently thought the same of Spago. "They came up to the kitchen," Puck said. "They'd never seen an open kitchen. They thought it was a buffet."

Once the cowboys left town, the pre-New Year's Eve doldrums didn't help matters. "In San Francisco and Los Angeles, December was the busiest time," Puck said. But things were different in Las Vegas. "They said it was the slow time, but I didn't think it would be that slow," he said. "I was really nervous. I had to go home and drink a bottle of wine in front of the TV to fall asleep, and then wake up at 6 in the morning with a headache and then go back and think about what I was going to do."

What he would do was stick it out and have a successful restaurant — one that's credited with starting the Las Vegas restaurant revolution, with Puck its leading patriot. And the state of Las Vegas dining would never be the same. "I think Las Vegas now has great restaurants," Puck said. "Restaurants and Cirque du Soleil are the main things in Las Vegas. Now restaurants have become a major tool of attracting people to Las Vegas." And how does Puck feel about that legacy?

"It doesn't make me feel bad," he said. "It's not that I'm going to take it to the grave."

As it turned out, other celebrity chefs had had their eye on the growth and development of Las Vegas in the early '90s but were waiting for someone to take the plunge. Once Puck jumped in with both feet, others started dipping in a toe.

"Then I brought Mark Miller here, and little by little …," Puck said. "I think then we had Emeril come. And then the Bellagio," with its full complement of restaurants run by celebrity chefs. The rest is culinary history.

Puck's road to Las Vegas began in one of the few countries that hasn't been featured in a Strip resort theme. He was born in St. Veit, Austria, to a hotel chef who cooked traditional Austrian cuisine and would serve to be a culinary inspiration for her son. Like most European chefs of his generation (Puck was born in 1949) he was apprenticed at a young age.

Starting at 14, he said, "mostly . . . was normal. If you learned a profession, it wasn't something unique that you started at 14. It sounds a little crazy now, because I have a son (Cameron) who is 14 years old. (Son Byron is about six years younger.) If he were to leave town to do an apprenticeship, I'd be so nervous."

Puck remembers those days as tough ones. "It was very difficult for kids who were 14 years old," he said. "All of a sudden, on Sunday morning, instead of going skiing, I had to go to work and cook. It wasn't really cooking, peeling potatoes and onions and hearing people yell at me. In the afternoon, I had to clean the stove in the kitchen. That's why I tell everybody 12 hours is only half a day."

Despite the slightly Dickensian beginnings of his career, Puck had found his niche. At age 17, he moved 1,000 miles away to France. He worked in France for seven years, at the three-star Hotel de Paris in Monaco, Maxim's in Paris and L'Oustau de Baumaniere in Provence.

But America was always in his thoughts. "Every young kid at that time dreamed of coming to America," he said. "Everybody thought in America, everybody's all right because they drive all those big cars. I was drawn from far away." Still, New York presented a bit of culture shock. "I didn't like it, because Paris is such a beautiful city and New York is so different," Puck said. "I didn't like the job I had in New York."

A friend got him a job in Indianapolis and told him about the auto races. "Indianapolis; that sounds great," Puck remembered thinking. He rode a Greyhound bus for two days. More culture shock: The young chef who'd worked in Paris and New York was quite unprepared for the prosaic American Midwest. On arrival, "I said, 'That's Indianapolis. Oh.' It didn't matter what I thought. I had no money left. I had to stay. I couldn't go back to New York or anything."

His Indianapolis sojourn would last only a year. The company that managed the restaurant, La Tour, lost its contract with Indiana National Bank. The company also, as it happened, managed a Los Angeles restaurant called Ma Maison. When Puck moved to Ma Maison, he said, it "at that time as a restaurant was nothing. Six months after, it started to do OK, and then it got better and better and better. "And in '82 we opened Spago," on the Sunset Strip in West Hollywood.

In the ensuing couple of decades, the Puck empire has grown to include, at press-time, 11 fine-dining restaurants, 45 casual and quick-service restaurants (with commitments for 165 more), a frozen-food line, canned soups, videos, and cookbooks. But Puck is philosophical about his phenomenal success.

"Doing well doesn't mean just having a lot of restaurants," he said. "Doing well means doing the right thing — training a lot of young people to do the right thing." He's extremely proud, he said, that his restaurants rank as the kind of places "where you would send your best friends to eat."

And he's still thinking ahead. "You have different dreams every night," Puck said. "There are certain things I'd like to do, and then I do them and it's no big deal. I want to be successful in Japan. I have three cafes and want to do an upscale restaurant there. I want to be successful in the frozen-food line, and canned soup. At the end of the day, for me the most important thing is that the customers are happy, and that they come back."

Wolfgang Puck's

PERSONAL FAVORITES

Postrio Baby Arugula Salad with Goat Cheese Fondue

Pumpkin Ravioli

Postrio Salmon en Papillote

Wolfgang Puck's

Postrio Baby Arugula Salad with Goat Cheese Fondue, D'anjou Pears, and Toasted Pecans

1 cup Goat Cheese Fondue (recipe follows)
12 spears endive
4 salad portions baby arugula (about 1 pound)
Salt
Freshly ground black pepper
⅛ cup fresh-squeezed lemon juice
¼ cup extra-virgin olive oil
1 d'Anjou pear, thinly sliced
¼ cup toasted pecan halves

Goat Cheese Fondue
⅔ cup soft goat cheese
½ cup heavy cream

Make goat cheese fondue and reserve in a warm-water bath.

Arrange the endive spears on 4 chilled plates (3 spears each).

Place arugula in a large mixing bowl and season lightly with salt and pepper. Add lemon juice and olive oil and toss until well coated, being careful not to bruise the lettuce. Place salad in equal portions on each plate.

Top each salad with sliced pear and pecans. Ladle 2 ounces of goat cheese fondue onto each salad and serve immediately.

Serves 4.

Goat Cheese Fondue: Crumble goat cheese into a small mixing bowl. Heat cream to near boil, reduce heat, and cook 1 minute. Remove and immediately add to bowl of goat cheese. Whisk out lumps.

Wolfgang Puck's

Pumpkin Ravioli

*¼ pound (1 stick) plus 2 tablespoons
unsalted butter (divided use)
1 pound fresh pumpkin, peeled, seeded and cut
into 1-inch cubes
2 cups heavy cream (divided use)
½ bay leaf
2 tablespoons minced fresh sage,
plus 6 small whole leaves for garnish
2 teaspoons minced fresh thyme leaves*

*3 eggs
Salt
Freshly ground white pepper
6 sheets (about 6 by 12 inches) fresh spinach pasta
¼ cup semolina or all-purpose flour, for dusting
2 cups chicken stock or good-quality chicken broth
2 shallots, chopped*

Heat a large, heavy skillet over low heat and add 4 tablespoons of the butter. When the butter is foamy, add the cubed pumpkin and cook, stirring often to prevent sticking and burning, until the pumpkin is tender, 15 to 20 minutes.

Transfer the pumpkin to a medium saucepan. Add 1 cup of the heavy cream, the bay leaf, and half of the sage and thyme and cook over low heat, stirring and mashing the pumpkin frequently with a wooden spoon, until it forms a thick puree with no excess liquid, about 30 minutes. If any lumps remain, use a fork to crush them into the mixture. Remove from the heat and beat in an additional 2 tablespoons butter.

Break 2 of the eggs into a small bowl and beat them thoroughly with the fork. Whisk the beaten eggs into the pumpkin. Season to taste with salt and pepper and set aside to cool.

On a floured work surface, lay out 3 sheets of pasta. Using a pastry bag or a tablespoon, place 8 equal mounds of the pumpkin puree on each sheet of dough, about 2 inches apart, using up all of the pumpkin puree. Break the remaining egg into a bowl and beat it lightly. Dip a pastry brush or your finger into the egg and use this egg wash to moisten the pasta evenly around each mound of filling. Cover each of the mounded dough sheets with a second sheet of pasta and press down around each mound of filling to seal the sheets of dough together.

Dust a tray or baking sheet with semolina. Using a 2-inch cookie cutter, cut out the ravioli, taking care to center the filling in each one and transferring each ravioli to the dusted tray as you cut it. Set the ravioli aside. Bring a large pot of salted water to a boil while you make the sauce.

Put the chicken stock and shallots in a medium saucepan. Over high heat, bring to a boil and

continue boiling until the liquid has reduced to ½ cup, about 15 minutes. Stir in the remaining 1 cup heavy cream and continue boiling until the liquid is reduced by half, 7 to 10 minutes. Reduce the heat to low and, a little at a time, whisk in the remaining 4 tablespoons butter. Strain the sauce into a clean saucepan, add the remaining sage and thyme, and season to taste with salt and pepper. Keep warm.

Add the ravioli to the rapidly boiling water and cook until al dente, 4 to 5 minutes. One by one, remove the ravioli with a slotted spoon, drain, and transfer to the sauce. Over medium heat, bring the sauce just back to a boil. Remove from the heat and adjust the seasonings to taste. Divide the ravioli among preheated plates and spoon the sauce over them. Garnish each serving with a fresh sage leaf. Serve immediately.

Serves 4.

Wolfgang Puck's

Postrio Salmon En Papillote

Olive oil
2 fennel bulbs, thinly sliced
Salt
Black pepper
2 parsnips, peeled, sliced thin on a bias
4 salmon fillets, 7 ounces each, skin and
pin bones removed
4 sheets thick parchment paper
(or substitute aluminum foil),
each about 18 by 24 inches
8 tablespoons shallot-herb butter
(recipe follows), softened

12 Roma tomato "petals"
(skinned, seeded, quartered Roma tomatoes
marinated lightly in olive oil, black pepper and salt)
8 tablespoons tomato sauce
(fresh, infused with basil and garlic)
8 sprigs chervil (omit if unavailable)
8 sprigs fresh dill
8 sprigs fresh Italian parsley
½ cup shallots, sliced thin
8 fingerling or Yukon Gold potatoes, blanched
in water until tender, peeled, and sliced
2 tablespoons melted butter

Shallot-Herb Butter
1 cup unsalted butter, softened
1 tablespoon chopped chervil (omit if unavailable)
1 tablespoon chopped dill
1 tablespoon chopped parsley
1 tablespoon finely chopped shallots
1 teaspoon lemon juice
1 ½ teaspoon salt
½ teaspoon black pepper

Prepare vegetables: Heat a medium saute pan to very hot, add 1 tablespoon olive oil, and carefully add half of the fennel. Season with salt and pepper and cook on high heat until tender and well caramelized. Remove to a sheet pan and spread thin to cool. Repeat process with second half of the fennel. Cool completely.

Repeat this process with the sliced parsnips. Set aside to cool.

Prepare fish: Season salmon fillets with salt and pepper and set aside.

Spread each piece of parchment onto open counter space. Realize that each piece will be folded in half lengthwise, and the fish will sit right near the crease. Approximately 1 inch from the where the crease will go, spread 1 tablespoon of shallot-herb butter on either side (in the center of the paper), so that when folded the butter will be both on the top and bottom of the fish.

In a small bowl, toss together the tomato petals, tomato sauce, and herb sprigs. Reserving 4 tablespoons of the mixture, place an even amount of remaining mixture on top of one side of the butter. Top this mixture with sliced shallots, potatoes, fennel, and parsnips, evenly dividing the vegetables for 4 portions.

Place each salmon fillet on top of the vegetables, and top with 1 tablespoon each of the reserved tomato-herb mixture.

Brush the melted butter on the outer 1-inch edge of the parchment. Fold the top half of the paper over the salmon until the edges meet, and roll the excess paper up toward the fillet to seal well (roll only about 1 inch of the paper up). Chill the salmon packages, or papillotes, for at least 20 minutes, or up to 4 hours.

Preheat oven to 500° F.

Remove papillotes from refrigerator 30 minutes before cooking. Place papillotes on two cookie sheets and bake in oven for 13 minutes. For medium rare salmon, bake for only 12 minutes. For well done, bake for 18 minutes. Do not be alarmed if the parchment paper browns well.

Serves 4.

For shallot herb butter: Combine all ingredients in a mixing bowl and mix well. Allow to stand at room temperature until ready to use.

Alessandro

Renoir

"I want [our customers] to have a world-class experience in my restaurant. Because we have all the tools. It's just a matter of sticking to it every day. We've got the best of the best."

When it comes to Renoir, his restaurant at the Mirage, Alessandro "Alex" Stratta changes with the weather. It's not that Stratta is wishy-washy, or that he has no vision, no clearly defined mission for his restaurant; quite the opposite. It's just that Stratta obtains about 80 percent of the produce used at Renoir from organic farms in Arizona and Utah, and so the menu is provided by the grace of Mother Nature. "I do whatever the weather dictates," Stratta said.

Why organic? "Flavor," he said simply. "There's a big difference in vegetables in the conversion from sugar to starch." As time passes, that means less sugar, more starch. Even a week after they've been picked, he said, organic products from nearby farms are "much better than what's in stores."

Using local organic produce also means he may have the luxury of choosing from among 40 varieties of heirloom tomatoes for the salads served at Renoir. "When you make tomato salads with everything organic, you can really discern the difference in flavor," Stratta said — especially since he keeps them simple, with just a little olive oil, salt, and pepper.

If it seems that Stratta takes particular pride of ownership regarding everything Renoir, know that he comes by it honestly. Stratta is from a fifth-generation hotel family. "I'm

*S*eating at Renoir can be a dicey proposition: If you face one of the master's works, you may find yourself gazing lovingly at it instead of your dining companion; if you face away from it, you may find yourself craning your neck. No matter, there's not a bad spot in the house. Yes, these are real Renoirs, but there are plenty of other touches that raise this intimate, classical restaurant a notch above even the best, such as plush banquettes, tiny stool-like platforms so ladies' handbags needn't touch the floor — even specialized lemon squeezers. It's an elegant island a coconut's throw (and half a world) from the casual tropical flavor of the Mirage. The menu is Franco-Italian and changes daily, taking advantage of the best — usually organic — of the market. Should availability be right, a house-cured salmon Napoleon would be a good place to start, continuing, maybe, with a roasted breast of pheasant with foie gras, potato, and artichoke confit. Dinner only. The Mirage, 3400 Las Vegas Blvd. South; 866-339-4566, or www.themirage.com.

not really from anywhere," he said. "I'm a hotel brat," raised in hotels until he was 14, and thereby also living on food from hotel dining rooms and room service.

We're not talking budget motels on the backroads of the America. Stratta was born in Pakistan, where his father was general manager at the Intercontinental Karachi. He lived in Indonesia, Malaysia, and Singapore, then in Mexico for almost

five years. Then the family moved to Rome, and then to the United States when Stratta was 10. He's fluent in French, Italian, and Spanish, as well as English.

Of his family, he said, "They've always been front-of-house people." Stratta, however, would gravitate toward the back. After graduating from the California Culinary Academy in San Francisco, he honed his baking skills at San Francisco's Stanford Court Hotel, then returned to Europe at age 20. He spent a few years at the Hotel de Paris in Monte Carlo, then moved on to

Alain Ducasse's Michelin three-star Louis XV. When Stratta returned to the United States, it was to work with Daniel Boúlud at Le Cirque in New York. Stratta is surely one of the few chefs in the United States who can claim both Ducasse and Boúlud — two lions of the culinary world — as mentors. "Both are very good friends," he said.

Stratta said he considers invaluable the experience he gained while working with Ducasse and Boúlud. And he still turns an eye toward his mentors, who continue to shape the state and future of American restaurants. "They are on the edge of transforming and introducing people to a different level of

restaurant," Stratta said. "Casual, medium-priced, but with the same phenomenal food." They are, he said, "very exacting people."

From Le Cirque, Stratta moved to the Phoenician in Scottsdale, Arizona, then owned by savings and loan financier Charles Keating. The move from New York to Phoenix might have seemed a bit unusual, but it was a chance for Stratta to run his own shop. "I think, at that point, I had nothing to lose," he said.

He spent the first three years running the now-legendary Mary Elaine's at the Phoenician. Then he took over the resort's Italian restaurant and ran both, and then was named executive chef for the hotel. He spent nine years at the Phoenician, helping to establish it as a five-star, five-diamond property, and in 1998 won a James Beard Foundation award, Best Chef: Southwest.

But, of course, new challenges awaited. "I needed another change," Stratta said. "I decided to look elsewhere." At about the same time, Las Vegas casino developer Steve Wynn was looking for top-notch chefs to shore up the restaurant offerings at his signature Mirage hotel-casino, which had opened in 1989. Stratta was offered an intimate room not far from the hotel's tropical atrium.

"It was called Melange," Stratta said. "It was a melange. It changed so many times that it confused everybody. It was hotel French food." But Stratta saw potential. He was excited about the size of the room — a quarter the size of his previous spot near Phoenix — and about the fresh-fish tanks in the back. "I came here to make it a great restaurant," he said. The confusion, however, would continue even after the space became Restaurant Alessandro Stratta. "People called it Melange a year after we opened," Stratta said. And it was lost in the shuffle of the openings of other, newer casinos — Mandalay Bay, Bellagio, the Venetian, and Paris all within the same time period.

One day, Stratta was given a message: "You gotta see the president" of the resort, he remembered. "I thought, 'Oh grrrrreat.'" But the news was welcome. "Do you mind if we call the restaurant 'Renoir'?" Stratta was asked. "The success of Picasso (at Bellagio) fueled it," he said.

In June 1999 the restaurant was closed, then re-opened as Renoir to capitalize on the originals that hang on its walls. Stratta sees the art in the dining room as an adjunct to the art he creates in the kitchen. "It's like nice china, but it costs a lot more," he said with a laugh.

Today, Stratta is sanguine about his contributions to the culinary revolution in Las Vegas, widely — and, just a few years ago, improbably — considered one of the best restaurant cities in the country. "I just came here to do great food and to establish Las Vegas as a place with great restaurants," Stratta said, adding that he wants to be "one of the people who make a difference in the culinary sense in Las Vegas."

And make a difference he has. Renoir and Picasso made history when they became the first Las Vegas restaurants to be graced with five stars by the Mobil Travel Awards program. Renoir ranks as one of the best restaurants in the city, and Stratta one of the best chefs — high praise considering that the top names in the culinary world continue to jockey for the prime spots in town.

Stratta said he welcomes the growing community of top-notch chefs and restaurants that the city has attracted. "It's very important to me to be surrounded with like-minded restaurateurs," he said. "It keeps us all going. This town doesn't ever seem to get oversaturated."

Stratta, who classifies Renoir as Franco-Italian, is a proponent of a return to a simpler approach to cooking. "I think it's important to go back to the basics," he said. "The basics of French and Italian cooking were always there. I like to always have a line to the classical cooking. Presentation is important, but flavor is number one for me. I'm very specific. If you order asparagus, you're going to taste asparagus." He believes in "very definitive, strong flavors."

Of his customers, he said, "I want them to have a world-class experience in my restaurant. Because we have all the tools. It's just a matter of sticking to it every day. We've got the best of the best."

Stratta said he appreciates Renoir's location. "Being in a casino is not a bad thing for a

restaurant," he said. "There's a continuous flow — not as many slow periods," and a network of concierges eager to cue their well-heeled clients to the best places in town. He also welcomes the financial support that comes with being a jewel in a casino's crown. "Where else can you get all the beautiful accoutrements?" Stratta asked.

He likes life in Las Vegas as well, and plans to stay awhile. "It took about three years to get used to living here," he said. "And the slow start here kind of soured it a little bit for me. But our life is great; we've made great friends."

"As a restaurateur, you can live here and have a wonderful life," Stratta said — for example, taking a drive with his wife to the scenic Red Rock Canyon National Conservation Area, only minutes from Las Vegas, on a balmy afternoon. "Seventy-one degrees in January is not bad," he said.

Despite all of his success, Stratta is not a household name, but he said he's happier that way than he would be with the very public fame that the mass media has brought the likes of Wolfgang Puck and Emeril Lagasse. Stratta says he's "a very reserved person. TV? It's just not me. Given the chance to be a star, a celebrity, I think I'd opt not to," he said, sitting in Renoir one afternoon, a masterwork on the wall over the master's head. "I'd rather just focus on what I do here."

♥

Alessandro Stratta's

PERSONAL FAVORITES

Ahi Carpaccio with Yellowtail and Caviar

Kobe Beef with Gnocchi

Lemon Meringue Tart

Alessandro Stratta's

Ahi Tuna Carpaccio with Yellowtail Tartare, Cucumbers, and Osetra Caviar

For the Potato Crisps:
1 Idaho potato, peeled
4 tablespoons clarified butter
Salt and pepper to taste

For the Ahi:
4 ounces fresh A-grade ahi tuna
1 teaspoon fresh yuzu juice
(or use 50-50 mixture of fresh lime
and orange juices, if yuzu juice
is not available)

1 tablespoon extra-virgin olive oil
Fleur de sel (sea salt) to taste
White pepper to taste

For the Yellowtail Tartare:
4 ounces fresh yellowtail (hamachi)
1 tablespoon yuzu vinaigrette (made
with 1 part yuzu juice, 3 parts extra-
virgin olive oil, and salt and pepper
to taste; use 50-50 mixture of
fresh orange and lime juices

if yuzu is unavailable)
Fleur de sel (sea salt) to taste
White pepper to taste
1 tablespoon minced chives

For the Garnish:
1 cup cucumber, peeled, seeded
and diced to ⅛-inch
Fleur de sel (sea salt) to taste
2 tablespoons crème fraiche
1 teaspoon fresh yuzu juice (or use 50-

50 mix of fresh lime and orange juices)
1 tablespoon minced chives
Fleur de sel (sea salt) to taste
White pepper to taste
½ cup cucumber slices
(very thin, skin on)
1 tablespoon mixed micro-greens
(frissee, chive, parsley, celery, etc.)
1 ounce golden Osetra caviar
1 tablespoon sliced mixed radishes

For potato crisps: Preheat oven to 300° F. Slice the peeled potato on a mandoline slicer Gaufrette-style (¹⁄₁₆-inch thick) and cut the slices with a 3-inch cookie cutter so they're all the same size. Place them on a flat sheet pan covered with a Silpat baking sheet brushed lightly with clarified butter, on the rough side of the Silpat, evenly spaced. Cover with another Silpat, on the smooth side, and bake for 15 to 20 minutes until evenly golden brown. Remove the slices, one at a time, and place them on a paper towel in a dry place until crisp and not too oily. Reserve at room temperature until needed.

For ahi carpaccio: Remove all sinew and otherwise nonusable portions of tuna and reserve the fish, chilled.

Place two layers of plastic wrap on a flat solid surface and place some of the tuna meat on top, covering with two additional layers of plastic.

Pound out lightly and evenly with the aid of a small meat mallet until ⅛-inch thick. With a 2 ½-inch cookie cutter, cut the pounded meat into rounds; reserve on a flat baking dish and repeat until you have five rounds of tuna per person, or 20 rounds.(Continue to reshape and pound the tuna to avoid any waste.) Refrigerate for up to two days.

For vinaigrette: Whisk yuzu juice with olive oil and salt and pepper to taste. Moments before serving, season and dress the ahi lightly with the yuzu vinaigrette.

For taretar: Remove all bloodlines and blemishes from the yellowtail, dice the fish into ¼-inch cubes, and reserve chilled. Moments before serving, dress with the yuzu vinaigrette and season with salt, pepper, and chives. Serve as soon as it is dressed.

For garnish: Place the diced cucumber in a

colander fitted with a piece of cheesecloth and season with salt. Refrigerate and allow to drain for 1 hour. Squeeze out all excess liquid and reserve the diced cucumber, discarding the liquid.

Mix the cucumber with the crème fraiche, yuzu juice, chives, and salt and white pepper to taste and reserve until needed.

To serve: dress both the diced yellowtail and the rounds of tuna with the vinaigrettes. Arrange the slices of cucumber around the inner circumference of a plate and follow with the rounds of dressed tuna. Place a dollop of the creamed cucumbers in the center and arrange a three-layered Napoleon of the yellowtail between layers of the potato crisps. Place the Napoleon on top of the cucumber salad and garnish with micro greens, caviar and radishes. Serve chilled.

Alessandro Stratta's

Kobe Beef with Potato Gnocchi, Parmigiano, and Bordelaise Sauce

For the Gnocchi:
8 large russet potatoes
2 cups kosher salt
1 ½ cups all-purpose flour
1 large egg

For the Steaks:
4 strip loin steaks (10 ounces each)
¼ cup extra-virgin olive oil
1 tablespoon fresh rosemary leaves
6 cloves of fresh garlic, thinly sliced
1 tablespoon black peppercorns,
coarsely ground

For the Red Wine Reduction:
2 tablespoons olive oil
3 pounds beef short rib scraps,
cut into 1-inch cubes
½ cup onions, finely diced
½ cup celery, finely diced
½ cup carrots, finely diced
2 heads of garlic, cut in half
1 bunch fresh thyme
12 black peppercorns
2 tablespoons red wine vinegar
2 bottles red Burgundy wine
1 gallon rich chicken stock

Finishing the Bordelaise Sauce:
2 tablespoons butter
4 tablespoons fresh beef bone marrow,
cut in ¼-inch dice (optional)
2 tablespoons shallots, diced
4 tablespoons Italian parsley,
(roughly chopped)
1 teaspoon coarse black pepper

For the Parmigiano Sauce:
1 cup dry white vermouth
¼ cup shallots, minced
1 tablespoon fresh thyme
1 cup chicken stock
2 tablespoons heavy cream
1 pound sweet butter, softened
Salt and pepper to taste
½ cup grated Parmigiano
1 tablespoon minced chives

For the gnocchi: Preheat oven to 350° F. Rinse and dry the potatoes well and place them on a baking sheet with a layer of salt as a base. Bake the potatoes for approximately 2 hours. Remove the potatoes and cut them in half; scoop out the pulp into a ricer while the pulp is still hot and rice the whole batch of potatoes. (If a ricer is unavailable, use a potato press, or pass through a colander.)

Sprinkle a clean work surface with flour. Place the pulp in a mound and poke a well in the middle; add the egg. Knead the dough lightly and add the remaining flour, a bit at a time, as you knead. Do not overwork the dough and always make while hot. Roll the dough into one homogeneous mass and cut in 6 even pieces. Take each piece and roll into a 1-inch tube about 18 inches long. Cut the tube into 1-inch pieces and roll each piece individually over a gnocchi paddle onto a floured sheet pan. (If a gnocchi paddle is not available, use the back of a fork or a butter curler.) Sprinkle flour lightly on top of the gnocchi once they are all completed. Reserve at room temperature in a dry place for up to six hours.

Cook in a large pot of simmering water (be sure not to crowd the gnocchi) about 30 to 45 minutes after gnocchi begin to float.

Makes enough for 20 servings. (To store extra, chill cooked gnocchi in ice water, drain, then place, separated, on an oiled surface, and freeze until needed.)

For the steaks: combine all ingredients except meat; marinate steaks in refrigerator at least overnight, but not longer than two days. Remove from marinade and season with Fleur de sel (sea salt) moments before searing.

For the red-wine reduction: preheat oven to 375° F. Heat a large heavy saucepan over high heat. Add the oil; allow it to get smoking hot and add the scraps in an even layer. Do not stir until the temperature reaches a high temperature again. Turn the pieces of beef over and color until dark brown; add the onions, celery, carrots, garlic heads, thyme, and peppercorns and continue to roast and color the vegetables lightly.

Drain any excess grease. Add wine vinegar to the pan and scrape up any brown bits. Add red wine, reduce by half, and add the stock. Bring to a boil and skim fat from top. Place in the oven for 3 hours, stirring occasionally. Strain through a fine mesh and skim off fat. Return to stove and reduce to 1 cup.

Simmer the sauce and swirl in the butter, then add marrow, shallots, parsley, and pepper. Simmer briefly. Season to taste.

For the Parmigiano sauce: place the vermouth, shallots, and thyme in a heavy saucepot and reduce until dry. Add the chicken stock and reduce to a glaze. Add the cream and simmer. Add the soft butter, a piece at a time, whisking until smooth. Season and strain. Keep in a warm place and finish with the cheese and the chives moments before serving.

Presenting the dish: Sear the seasoned steaks over high heat and cook to the desired temperature (suggest rare to medium-rare). Allow meat to rest in a warm spot for 2 to 3 minutes before carving.

For each serving, place ¼ cup of the Parmigiano sauce in a pan and place 5 to 6 gnocchi gently in the sauce.

Arrange the gnocchi and sauce on a plate. Place a pool of Bordelaise sauce on the plate. Slice the beef into long thin slices and fan them out on the plate. Drizzle gnocchi with the Bordelaise sauce and the meat with the Parmigiano sauce. Serve hot.

Serves 4.

Alessandro Stratta

Lemon Meringue Tart

For the lemon curd:
3 whole eggs
3 egg yolks
1 ½ cups granulated sugar
1 ½ cups fresh lemon juice
1 stick sweet unsalted butter
(cold, cut in small cubes)

For the lemon soufflé base:
2 eggs, separated
¼ cup fresh lemon juice
¾ teaspoon fresh grated lemon zest
3 tablespoons sugar, divided use
1 ½ teaspoons cornstarch
12-inch sugar-dough crust, 1 inch high,
pre-baked and cooled
Raspberry sauce

For the lemon curd: in a bowl, combine the eggs, yolks, and sugar. Whisk until smooth; add the lemon juice and whisk briskly.

Place the bowl over a pan of simmering water and whisk until mixture begins to thicken. Remove from the flame and allow to thicken at room temperature. Add the diced cold butter, a little at a time, until incorporated. Strain through a fine strainer and cool in the refrigerator for 2 hours.

For the lemon soufflé base: place the egg yolks, lemon juice, zest, and 2 tablespoons sugar in a bowl and whisk until smooth. Add the cornstarch in a slow, steady stream, whisking until smooth and avoiding lumps. Reserve until needed.

To make meringue mixture, whisk the egg whites with the remaining 1 tablespoon of sugar until soft peaks form. Gently fold in ½ cup of the lemon soufflé base and set aside.

Line the bottom of the cooled, pre-baked crust with a thin layer of the lemon curd and set aside.

Pre-heat oven to 450° F. Place the lemon meringue mixture in a piping bag fitted with a tip of your choice and pipe meringue into the tart directly over the curd. Pipe out until thick and 2 ½ inches high. Bake in a pre-heated oven for 6-8 minutes until lightly browned. The center should still be cold, and the meringue hot. Serve immediately, with raspberry sauce of your choice.

Serves 6.

(Recipe from Renoir pastry chef Jennifer White.)

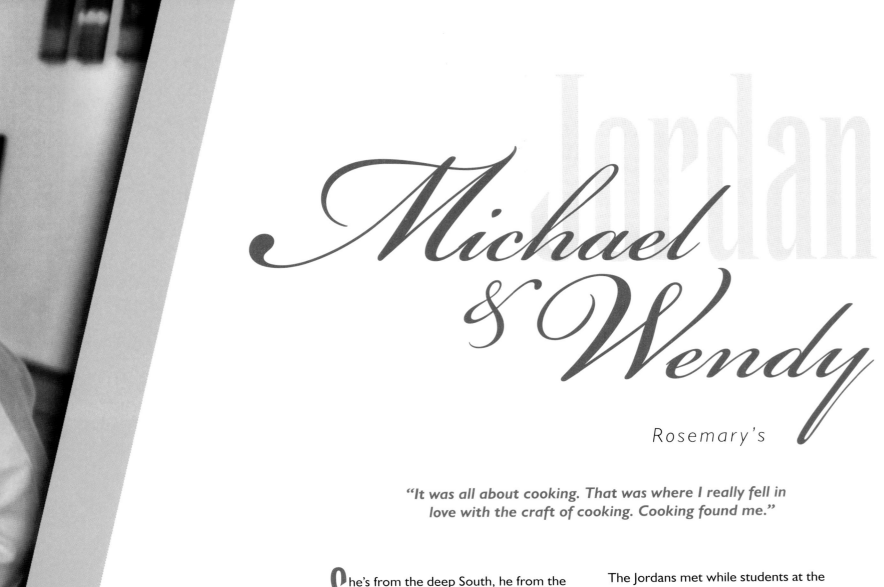

Michael & Wendy *Jordan*

Rosemary's

"It was all about cooking. That was where I really fell in love with the craft of cooking. Cooking found me."

She's from the deep South, he from the heart of the Heartland. They spent three months traveling Europe together, then made a circuit of the USA. And all of it shows in the menus of Michael and Wendy Jordan's Rosemary's Restaurant, which are characterized by diverse flavors held together by an American regional theme.

The Jordans met while students at the prestigious Culinary Institute of America in Hyde Park, New York, but their routes to Hyde Park were as different as their backgrounds. A native of Nebraska who was raised in Iowa, Michael Jordan dropped in and out of college a few times before deciding that it wasn't for him; he had no

patience for required courses that were of no interest. And his first job — at a McDonald's outlet, when he was 16 — had been immensely attractive because of the sense of family that comes with working in a restaurant.

But he wasn't dreaming of a toque of his own. "Growing up in Iowa, you don't think about being a chef," he said; he was a cook, which "was kind of like being an auto mechanic." His mother, who saw the joy he found in the kitchen, suggested a cooking school. They took a trip to the Hyde Park campus. "I want to go here," he remembered saying. "It was all about cooking. That was where I really fell in love with the craft of cooking. Cooking found me."

For Wendy Jordan, the path was more direct. "I just got it in my head that what I wanted to do was cook," she said. She was born in Mississippi and grew up in New Orleans and Houston. "Mom and Dad took us out to eat a lot," she said. "I learned all about the art of dining." Pretty soon cooking was a hobby. "Whenever I was bored," she said, "what I would do is cook."

She came by her cooking skills honestly. Each summer, she'd stay with her father in Mississippi, where her stepmom taught her how to put up tomatoes and make jam, jellies, pickles, and chowchow. "So I was exposed to the fine side of life, and country-style," she said.

After high school, she entered restaurant school at the University of Houston — where a French chef promptly did his best to talk her out of her chosen career, telling her, "You'll never have a family. You'll never have children." She said she walked away from cooking mentally — for a while. It wasn't long before she decided, "Screw this. I'm just going to go and see what happens. Luckily, I had the drive."

Rosemary's West Sahara Avenue location is slipped into a strip mall, but don't let that fool you; inside, the mood is gracious. The open space feels elegant, but details like the large, color-splashed, post-modern paintings and up-to-the-minute draped-glass lighting fixtures give it a contemporary feel. The restaurant is fronted by a bar that's a popular early-evening gathering spot, and the kitchen is open to view; stop by and you might see Michael or Wendy Jordan peering out to check things in the dining room. If you pause at noon, you'll see ladies who lunch joined by Las Vegas' ruling class, who stop by to greet each other as they come in for a power lunch. Try the Hugo's Texas BBQ Shrimp with Maytag Blue Cheese Coleslaw and you'll gain a new appreciation for the Jordans' melding of their Southern and Midwest roots. Lunch and dinner. Rosemary's Restaurant, 8125 W. Sahara Ave.; 702-869-2251, or www. rosemarysrestaurant.com.

She eventually decided to go to the CIA as well. And when the two reflected on their education, they firmly agreed on one point: At the CIA, they learned to cook. "It is the Harvard of trade schools," Chef Mike said.

They graduated in 1989. But their education wasn't finished. They moved to Iowa City, Iowa, and took jobs in a restaurant called The Kitchen. It was, he said, "one of the greatest jobs ever." Their marching orders from the owner: "Cook anything you want." They were ready. At CIA, Chef Wendy said, "they crammed so much into your head, and we just started pulling it out."

As they worked, they saved their money, a grand tour of Europe in mind. By April 1990, they were ready. They didn't do any formal food-related schooling in Europe, but "anything that was food-related, we gravitated toward," Chef Mike said. "In a real roundabout way, it was really a cook's tour."

Then it was back to Iowa City and the kitchen at The Kitchen. It was, he said, at a time when ingredients like fresh herbs and whole salmon were getting easier to find. "People were just waking up to food nationwide."

"If the owner of that restaurant could've kept us forever, she'd have been the happiest person in the world," Chef Wendy said.

But by 1991 it was time to move on. "We had gone to Europe, so we wanted to see America," Chef Mike said. They went to Alaska, followed the West Coast,

then to Houston and were on their way to Atlanta when they decided to drive through New Orleans. By the time they got there, they'd made a decision. "The first 'For Rent' sign we see, we're stopping," Chef Mike remembered saying.

The first sign they saw — for an apartment over a rather raucous bar — had a note, "See Bartender." The bartender, a woman named Rocket, was blunt: "You don't want it." They did, though, and the apartment would provide some interesting stories — like the time Rocket pulled a gun and went after a misbehaving customer while Chef Wendy's grandmother sat nearby, sipping her morning coffee.

They set their sights high. "We were going to work in one of the top five restaurants in the city, or we were going to move on," Chef Mike said.

"You have to find your own personal mentor, hone your skills, and then go off on your own," Chef Wendy said. They went to see Susan Spicer, who had earned respect with her restaurants Bayona, Herbsaint, and Cobalt. Spicer didn't have any spots but sent them on to Emeril Lagasse, who, as it turned out, had just fired one of his chefs the day before. Chef Mike had a spot on the line. "I was not allowed to cook food for eight months," he remembered.

Chef Wendy still wanted to work for Spicer and hopped from job to job while she waited for an opening. She eventually went to work

for Spicer and stayed two years. She also was working part-time at Peristyle, and "I fell in love with Peristyle," she said; she stayed three years. Eventually, chef/owner John Neal asked her to work for him full time. She became Neal's sous chef. When Neal fell ill, she found herself running the restaurant, continuing for about six months after his death.

In the fall of 1995, Lagasse asked Chef Mike to move to Las Vegas to open Emeril's at the MGM Grand. Chef Wendy followed in February 1996. He stayed at Emeril's for about two years, while she ran "this little catering thing," she said.

They'd been thinking about opening their own restaurant, but he was determined to take a break to spend some time with their son, then 2. They started lining up financing. Friends and family chipped in a lot, he said, but it still wasn't enough. "Banks in general don't want to give money to restaurants," he said, "and I don't blame them" because of the high failure rate nationwide. Frustrated, "I was thinking about going back to Emeril," he said.

Then serendipity intervened. A steady customer, a man from Chicago who had dined at the kitchen table at Emeril's five to six times a year, heard the Jordans were thinking of opening a restaurant and needed a backer. He called and offered to help. "We had a restaurant," Chef Mike said. "He gave us what we needed to get that loan."

Rosemary's Restaurant opened in May 1999. The opening wasn't without pitfalls;

Chef Wendy found herself crying at the local power company. And there would be more to come. "That first year is a bear," Chef Mike said. "It was a monster. The office side was the learning curve for me."

"You start to feel empathy for your former bosses," Chef Wendy said.

Still, they'd expand Rosemary's just eight months after it opened — and serendipity would again play a role. A storefront next to the restaurant had become available, and the couple decided to grab it while they could. Their accountant told them, "Don't do this. You are insane." But the risk paid off. "It's been, in the long term, one of the smartest moves we've made," Chef Mike said.

More and more people were finding Rosemary's, and many of them became loyal regulars. One was legendary chef Jean-Louis Palladin, who had a home nearby, and whose Napa would become Rosemary's at the Rio about a year after his death. The Jordans would close the Rio location about a year later.

But they still feel the legacy of Palladin, widely regarded as one of a handful of chefs who helped Americans rise to a new level of gastronomy, through his restaurants in Washington, D.C., and Las Vegas.

"I believe that we understood Jean-Louis," Chef Mike said. "I think we hold the same goal in mind. I think our crowd is very diverse. I love that about it. That's one I

take a lot of pride in. We have a message that does touch over a broad range."

The Jordan family includes two young children. "If there's one thing that our kids know, it's that they're loved," he said. There's lots of love to go around, it seems. Chef Wendy's mother, Maggie Bock, handled public relations for the restaurant for the first few years. Rosemary's was named for Chef Mike's mother "because she didn't give up on me at a time when I think everybody else had," he said. "I don't think I would ever be doing this if she had given up."

"We didn't open the restaurant until we believed we had something to say," he said. Through the restaurant, "I'm trying to tell you about our life. It took us a long time to realize that this is what we wanted to say."

◆

Michael & Wendy Jordan's

PERSONAL FAVORITES

Prosciutto-Wrapped Cheese-Stuffed Figs

Honey-Grilled Wild King Salmon on Apple-Fennel Slaw

Lemon Ice Box Pie with Raspberry Sorbet

Michael & Wendy Jordan's

Prosciutto-wrapped Cheese-Stuffed Figs
with Vanilla-arugula Pesto and Balsamic Extraction

For Stuffed Figs:
*About 9 ounces Sonoma goat cheese
plus extra for garnish
9 figs
Salt
White pepper
18 paper-thin slices Prosciutto
di Parma
12 ounces Pesto Sauce (recipe follows)
3 tablespoons Balsamic Extraction*

*1 cup loosely packed arugula
3 tablespoons Vanilla Bean Oil
(recipe follows)
6 whole basil leaves, cut in chiffonade
(thin ribbon-like strips)*

For Pesto Sauce:
*3 cloves garlic
2 ounces pine nuts, toasted
1 cup extra-virgin olive oil*

*3 ½ ounces spinach, blanched
and squeezed
3 cups tightly packed fresh
basil leaves, blanched and squeezed
4 ounces Parmesano Reggiano, grated
2 ounces Pecorino Romano, grated
1 teaspoon white pepper
Salt to taste
(cheeses are naturally salty)*

For Balsamic Extraction:
*1 quart balsamic vinegar
½ cup orange juice
¼ cup honey*

For Vanilla Bean Oil
*1 vanilla bean
1 quart peanut oil*

For stuffed figs: Preheat oven to 350° F. Divide goat cheese into 18 portions and roll each into a ball. Slice each fig in half and place a ball of cheese in the middle. Gently press it into the flesh of the fig and season with salt and white pepper. Fold the prosciutto in half lengthwise and wrap the prosciutto around the fig with the ends hidden under the fig. Lay all figs, cheese side up, on an oiled cookie sheet and bake briefly until the prosciutto begins to turn golden brown.

To serve: pool some of the pesto sauce in the middle of six warm plates and lay the figs (3 halves per plate) with the fat ends toward the center in a star-like pattern. (Leave a small gap in the center for the arugula.) Put the balsamic extraction in a squeeze bottle and outline the pesto pool with it to keep the oil from separating. Toss the arugula with the vanilla oil, season with salt and white pepper, and pile it in the center of the figs. Sprinkle with

the basil. Crumble just a tiny bit of the goat cheese around. Be sure to serve figs warm.

Serves 6.

For pesto sauce: Put the garlic and pine nuts in a food processor and run for 1 minute. Add the oil slowly, and then add the spinach and basil. Run for 4 minutes. Add the cheeses and pepper and run for 2 minutes. Taste for seasoning and smoothness. (Sauce will be very thick; it can be thinned with more extra-virgin olive oil.) Makes 2 cups.

For balsamic extraction: Place all ingredients in a medium saucepot and slowly bring to a boil. Reduce heat so that there is no motion to the mixture — only steam wafting off of the surface (it will take quite a while to reduce, maybe 4 to 5 hours or longer). The slower the reduction, the less chance

of burning the natural and added sugars. Be sure to skim off any scum that forms on the surface of the mixture as it reduces. To test if it is done, place a small plate in the freezer for 5 minutes. Spoon a teaspoon or more of the mixture onto the plate and swirl gently. You will see whether it is thick enough, as it should be like honey. Continue to reduce, if necessary. Makes ¼ to ½ cup.

For vanilla bean oil: Split 1 whole vanilla bean in half. Place 1 quart of peanut oil in a small saucepot. Scrape the inside of the vanilla bean into the pot and add the pod. Place on low heat and warm slowly. Check the temperature of the oil with your finger to be sure it never becomes hotter than warm to the touch; if the oil becomes too hot, it will kill the flavor of the vanilla. Once it is warm, remove it from the stove and cool to room temperature. Pour into a bottle, adding the vanilla bean, and cap tightly. Makes 1 quart. Reserve extra for other uses.

Michael & Wendy Jordan's

Honey-grilled Wild King Salmon on Apple-fennel Slaw with Toasted Walnut Vinaigrette

For Salmon Marinade:
½ cup plus 2 tablespoons loosely
packed fresh basil leaves, blanched
and chopped
¼ cup preserved lemon, chopped
1 quart peanut oil
1 teaspoon white pepper, ground

For Salmon:
½ cup peanut oil
4 6-ounce portions wild King salmon,
marinated 2 hours to 3 days
Salt
White pepper

For slaw:
1 Granny Smith apple, peeled
and quartered
About 2 cups green cabbage,
shaved thin
¼ fennel bulb, shaved thin
¼ cup Walnut Vinaigrette
(recipe follows)
2 tablesppons green onions,
shaved thin
Salt
White pepper

For Walnut Vinaigrette:
¾ cup walnuts
1 shallot, finely diced
2 tablespoons honey
½ cup cider vinegar
2 cups peanut oil
1 cup walnut oil
2 tablespoons chives, minced
Salt and white pepper to taste

For Candied Walnuts:
4 egg whites
1 tablespoon water
1 ½ cups sugar
1 teaspoon salt
1 teaspoon cinnamon
2 cups walnut nuggets

For serving:
1 cup Walnut Vinaigrette
½ cup honey (the best quality possible)
½ cup Candied Walnuts
4 tablespoons Port Wine Syrup

For Port Wine Syrup
½ bottle Port wine

For salmon marinade: Using a blender, combine the basil, lemon, 1 cup of the peanut oil, and the white pepper and puree very well. Add the puree to the remaining oil and stir well. Marinate 2 hours to 3 days. Makes 1 quart.

For salmon: Use two large sauté pans. Add just enough peanut oil to cover the bottom of each pan and place over medium heat. Season the marinated salmon to taste with salt and white pepper and when the oil smokes, add the salmon to the pans. Leave them alone until a good crust forms, then turn them over. Cook to medium rare (or your preferred degree of doneness) then remove to a plate, cover, and keep warm until needed.

For slaw: Grate the Granny Smith apple and, in a medium bowl, combine with the cabbage, fennel, walnut vinaigrette, and green onions. Toss well and season with salt and white pepper. Taste and adjust seasoning if necessary.

For walnut vinaigrette: Toast walnuts at 325° F until golden brown. Meanwhile, combine the shallot, honey, and vinegar in a blender. Turn blender on and slowly add the oils. Pour vinaigrette over the warm walnuts and stir in the chives. Taste and season with salt and white pepper. Makes 1 quart.

For candied walnuts: Preheat oven to 225° F. Beat egg whites with the water just to loosen the whites. Add the sugar and seasonings and stir well to combine. Roll nuts in the mixture and spread onto an oiled sheet of parchment paper on a cookie sheet. Bake 1 hour, stirring every 15 minutes. Once they are done, remove from the oven and stir again as they cool to coat the nuts completely with the mixture. Cool before storing. Makes 2 cups.

Port Wine Syrup: Place ½ bottle Port wine in a saucepot and reduce slowly until wine is thick, like a syrup. To check, place a small plate in the freezer for 5 minutes and drizzle a bit of the syrup onto the plate. If it does not run, it is done. Makes about ¼ cup.

To serve: Using four warm entrée plates, ladle ¼ cup of Walnut Vinaigrette onto each plate. Place the slaw in the middle of the plate. Top the slaw with the salmon. Drizzle each portion of salmon with a little of the honey and sprinkle with the candied walnuts and a little of the Port wine syrup.

Serves 4.

Michael & Wendy Jordan's

Lemon Ice Box Pie with Raspberry Sorbet, Vanilla Whipped Cream, and Raspberry Coulis

For Pie:
1 ½ cups lemon juice
1 cup sugar
3 teaspoons unflavored gelatin
1 ½ cups sweetened condensed milk
1 10-inch Graham Cracker Crust, cooled
(recipe follows)

For Whipped Cream:
2 cups heavy cream
½ cup sugar
2 teaspoons vanilla extract

To Serve:
2 cups Raspberry Coulis (recipe follows)
8 scoops Raspberry Sorbet (recipe follows)
1 tablespoon powdered sugar, for sprinkling

For Graham Cracker Crust:
1 cup graham cracker crumbs
1/2 teaspoon cinnamon, ground
½ cup sugar
8 tablespoons butter (1 stick), melted

For Raspberry Coulis:
½ cup sugar
¼ cup water
½ pound fresh raspberries
1 ½ teaspoons fresh lemon juice

For Raspberry Sorbet:
5 pounds raspberries, frozen
2 cups sugar
¼ cup water
1 tablespoon vodka

For pie: Put the lemon juice and sugar in a saucepan. Heat the juice mixture over medium heat, stirring, until the sugar dissolves, then bring to a boil.

Meanwhile, put the gelatin in a bowl and when the juice mixture boils, pour over the gelatin and whisk well, making sure all gelatin is dissolved. Add the sweetened condensed milk and mix well. Pour into prepared crust and chill until set, at least 4 hours.

For whipped cream: Put the heavy cream in the bowl of a stand mixer. Begin whipping and after 10 seconds slowly add the sugar and vanilla. Whip on medium speed until the cream forms peaks. Taste and adjust to your liking.

For graham cracker crust: Preheat oven to 325° F. Combine all ingredients except the butter in a food processor and run for 10 seconds to mix. Slowly pour in the butter. Mix for 30 seconds and test in your hand; if crumbs hold together when squeezed in your palm, they are moist enough. Taste for flavor.

Press into a 10-inch pie tin and bake for 10 to 15 minutes, or until just beginning to turn golden brown and very fragrant. Makes 1 10-inch crust.

For raspberry coulis: Combine all ingredients in a small saucepan and bring to a boil, allowing the sugar to dissolve before boiling. Simmer 5 minutes; puree and strain through a fine-meshed strainer. Chill and check consistency. Thin with a little water

if coulis is too thick. Makes 2 cups.

For raspberry sorbet: Place all ingredients in a large saucepot, bring to a boil slowly to allow the sugar to dissolve properly, and cook 5 minutes. Puree and pass through a fine strainer. Chill in an ice bath and run in an ice-cream machine. Makes 2 quarts.

To serve: Place ¼ cup raspberry coulis on a large entrée plate. Slice the lemon pie into 8 pieces and remove 1 wedge and place in the center. Put a scoop of raspberry sorbet on top and dollop with whipped cream over the sorbet. Sprinkle with powdered sugar.

Serves 8.

David Robins

Spago

In this day and age, if you are not a combination of a chef and a businessman, you will fail."

After a lifetime in San Francisco, Las Vegas wasn't exactly what David Robins had in mind. Robins actually is a native of Athens, Ohio, a college town in the rolling Appalachian foothills in the southeastern part of the state. But when he was just a tot, his family moved to San Francisco, and Robins grew up and began his professional life there.

Culinary school? He didn't need no stinkin' culinary school; Robins is a proud self-proclaimed graduate of the School of Hard Knocks. And that was a school to which he dedicated a PhD.'s worth of study.

Robins first learned to cook in his mother's kitchen, but much of his inspiration came

from the city's wealth of culinary treasures. "Growing up in San Francisco, I was able to have bountiful good cuisine," he said.

He didn't plan to make chefdom his life's work. His boyhood dream had been to play left field for the San Francisco Giants, and when he won a baseball scholarship to San Francisco State University, it seemed he was on his way. When that didn't work out, he turned to broadcasting. He studied TV and radio in college and worked in radio in San Francisco for four years.

But while the big leagues of baseball didn't come calling, the big leagues of

the culinary world would. Robins started slowly, but success loomed large.

He first fell in love with cooking, he said, "because I needed a job when I was in school." He went to work at Jeremiah Tower's Santa Fe Bar & Grill, under the tutelage of Chef Mark Franz. "He was more my mentor" than Tower, Robins said of Franz.

He moved with Franz to Stars, in all spending 11 years at Tower restaurants. But by the dawn of the '90s, Robins was ready for a change. At Stars, he happened to cook for David and Annie Gingrass, chefs at Postrio in San Francisco. The Gingrasses were impressed, and coincidentally, Robins had just given notice.

They asked: "Have you ever thought about moving to Las Vegas?"

"I said 'no.' "

"Would you?"

"No."

A few days later, David Gingrass called Robins and told him Wolfgang Puck wanted to meet him. "We talked about food and life and each other," Robins remembered. Their philosophies and work ethics clearly were compatible. Robins

went to Postrio as sous chef in 1991. "I quietly proved myself after about a month," Robins said.

He moved on to the Los Angeles area, working at the West Hollywood Spago, Granita, and Chinois. In 1992, he opened

Spago is, you might say, the Garden of Eden — the genesis of the Las Vegas restaurant revolution, opening in 1992 at the Forum Shops at Caesars. A $1 million renovation in 2001 only lifted the spirits of Spago's sleek, post-modern interior (the first Las Vegas design by Adam Tihany), and it remains one of the premier dining spots in town. Spago's open-air café overlooking the Forum Shops' shopping promenade remains one of the premier people-watching spots in Las Vegas; its dining room offers a little more privacy. The well-varied cafe menu includes many of the gourmet pizzas that helped make Wolfgang Puck a household name, plus what many regard as the best meatloaf in town. David Robins has directed more elegant offerings in the dining room, such as veal sweetbreads with eggplant Parmesan and prosciutto, or grilled free-range chicken with potato puree, baby vegetables, and Port wine sauce. Lunch and dinner are served in the café, dinner only in the dining room. Puck's other Las Vegas restaurants are Trattoria del Lupo at Mandalay Bay, Postrio in the Grand Canal Shoppes at the Venetian, Chinois in the Forum Shops, and the Wolfgang Puck Bar & Grill at the MGM Grand. Spago, the Forum Shops at Caesars, 3500 Las Vegas Blvd. South; 702-369-6300 or www.wolfgangpuck.com.

Spago Las Vegas. "I was very, very skeptical" about Las Vegas, Robins said. "I basically made a one-year deal. I was slightly intimidated by a city I didn't know much about." But he was impressed by managing partner Tom Kaplan — and of course by Puck — and saw the move as an opportunity to find a niche. "I took a leap," he said. A temporary one, he figured. Robins thought San Francisco would always be his home.

Spago Las Vegas made a slow start — very slow, because the opening was in December, traditionally a low month for Las Vegas tourism. "I thought I'd made the biggest mistake of my life," Robins said. But the restaurant rapidly found an eager clientele and did $12 million in business the first year. "I'd worked in big restaurants, but I'd never seen volume or business like this," Robins said.

The wild success of Spago prompted him to stay on after that first year. After two years he approached Puck about becoming a partner. He expected Puck to turn him down, and was prepared to move on. But, Robins said, Puck readily agreed.

For the first couple of years, he said, Spago's clientele was mainly tourists, people who knew Puck's restaurants from their exposure in other cities. And while the Forum Shops' location on the Strip pretty much means it will remain a hot spot for the out-of-town crowd, Robins is proud that the local clientele has grown to about 20 percent of business. He's also proud that many of those locals have become Spago regulars.

Robins has found a niche and a new home. "Vegas has been extremely good to me," he said. He's been good to it in return, serving on the board of directors of Big Brothers and Big Sisters of Southern Nevada and contributing to the work of the Arthritis Foundation, the Alzheimer's Foundation, and the March of Dimes.

Robins has found himself not only part of a community but part of a movement as well. He sees Las Vegas today as a dining destination that can compete with New York and, yes, San Francisco. And he's been more than happy to welcome the celebrity chefs who have followed in Spago's wake. In the early days, he said, many of the chefs contemplating a move to Las Vegas came to talk to Robins first.

"That's what I missed the first year — the chefs' community," he said. He certainly has that now, and he frequents many of those chefs' restaurants. Robins said Nobu is his favorite Las Vegas restaurant, and he considers Alessandro Stratta of Renoir at the Mirage to be Las Vegas' best chef.

Puck's interests in Las Vegas have continued to grow. The Wolfgang Puck Fine Dining Group now has five restaurants in Las Vegas and a growing catering business. The catering arm alone does about $5 million in gross sales, serving groups of 10 to 5,000. "We're all under the umbrella of Wolfgang Puck," Robins said.

And the Las Vegas fine-dining and catering businesses are under the umbrella of

David Robins. There's always a lot of debate among those trying to define the restaurants' contemporary appeal. Robins characterizes the local restaurants this way:

- ♠ Spago: California cuisine with an Asian influence.

- ♠ Trattoria del Lupo (Mandalay Bay): Originally regional Southern Italian, but now "re-accessible" with re-invented classics. "I learned a lesson down there about being too specific," Robins said with characteristic candor.

- ♠ Chinois (Forum Shops at Caesars): Asian with a French flavor. It has evolved to "things that people realize from classic Chinese food," more Hong Kong-style Chinese food, as well as classic Japanese sushi. Robins said Chinois "leans toward a classic Chinese restaurant that's hip and young."

- ♠ Postrio (The Venetian): "American with French influence, and more of an affiliation with Spago."

At all of them, Robins remembers the importance of accessibility. "I don't want to be perceived as a special-occasion restaurant," he said; and indeed the more casual cafes at Spago and Postrio are a means to that end. "If you cook with the best ingredients and do it well, you'll be successful," he said. "I never got into this business to be the next Paul Bocuse," one of the founders of nouvelle cuisine. At the same time, Robins recognizes the importance of raising the bar

for the American public. "I really believe it's about education," he said. "It's an information and sales job — to help people try things."

The education of the group's 600 Las Vegas employees is important to him as well. Robins is proud of the fact that alumni of Spago Las Vegas have moved up to lead the restaurants in the Las Vegas group, and that he's sent chefs to Puck restaurants in Palo Alto, California, and Maui.

For the first five years, he said, he cooked every night, but now he considers his role primarily management. "I don't consider myself that talented culinarily," Robins said. "In my day, I was a great line cook. I'm a great organizer." His role, he said, is similar to that of the manager of a baseball team, and as a representative to the public "in a mini-Wolf fashion." But he sometimes misses the kitchen. "It was a live performance," Robins said. "Every day, the curtain went up. I don't get that satisfaction anymore. My problems roll from day to day."

He said he has no regrets about not attending culinary school, but does regret that he didn't spend a concentrated year in Europe in his early days. "I definitely wish I had gone to business school and taken psychology classes. In this day and age, if you are not a combination of a chef and a businessman, you will fail."

Robins said he tries to get to each of the restaurants every night, sometimes wearing chef's whites, sometimes a business suit,

to bridge the parts of his business. As you might imagine, that requires a lot of hours. Robins figures he works about 14 hours a day, six days a week. "I do this because it's a lifestyle," he said.

And he's happy to labor in relative obscurity — at least relative to Wolfgang Puck. A "Best Chef" award that plastered his photo on the cover of a local magazine was a little unnerving, Robins said. As far as becoming a household name himself, "I have no desire to," Robins said. "Wolf is the brand name. Wolf is the icon. I value my personal time — what little time I have. We're not in an ego battle. We do this together. I have no problem making Wolf look good. That's what I consider to be my job. I'm honored that he has allowed me to do that for him. I'm all about being rich, not famous."

His feelings toward Las Vegas now, more than a decade later? "I'm entrenched," Robins said. "I can't believe I'm saying this, but I love Las Vegas now." And then, with a sardonic laugh, the spirit of a true Las Vegan: "Or at least I'm used to it."

David Robins'

Lobster Salad with White Truffle Vinaigrette

Foie Gras with Sauteed Apples

Mesquite Grilled Côte de Boeuf

David Robins'

Lobster Salad with White Truffle Vinaigrette

For salad:
1 pound trimmed green beans
6 braised artichoke hearts–cut in sixths
3 ripe Roma tomatoes, cut in sixths
3 lobster tails, steamed and
cut in 1-inch medallions

For vinaigrette:
1 tablespoon Champagne vinegar
1 tablespoon Dijon mustard
¼ cup olive oil
¼ cup peanut oil
2 tablespoons truffle oil
1 shallot, finely chopped
10 sprigs Italian parsley, stems removed,
finely chopped
Salt to taste
White pepper to taste

Boil green beans for 2 minutes in salted boiling water and then immediately place in ice water. Strain and set aside.

For the vinaigrette: In a mixing bowl, whisk the vinegar with the mustard; slowly drizzle in all of the oils so as not to break the vinaigrette (it's best to do it with two people). Add shallot and parsley, and salt and pepper to taste.

To prepare the salad: In a bowl, toss the artichokes, beans, and tomatoes with enough vinaigrette to moisten. Mound on the plate. Place lobster medallions on top and drizzle with additional vinaigrette.

Serves 4.

David Robins'

Foie Gras with Sauteed Apples

1 duck liver
2 small Granny Smith or Pippin apples
Juice of ½ lemon
5 tablespoons unsalted butter (divided use)
Salt
Freshly ground pepper
1 tablespoon flour
2 tablespoons almond or safflower oil
½ cup Port
1 tablespoon green peppercorns, rinsed

Clean the liver of all nerves and vessels that may be attached. Cut into ⅜-inch slices.

Peel and core the apples. Cut them into thin slices, about ¼ inch. Toss with the lemon juice and set aside.

Heat a sauté pan. Add 2 tablespoons of the butter and sauté the apples until they are slightly brown but still slightly crunchy. Transfer the apples to a plate and keep warm.

Melt the remaining 2 tablespoons of butter in the same pan with the oil. Season the liver slices with salt and pepper and dip them lightly in the flour.

Saute them over high heat for about 30 seconds on each side. The liver slices should be medium-rare, no more. (Saute the livers in separate batches so they are not crowded.) Transfer to a warm plate.

Deglaze the pan with the Port, stir in the peppercorns, then reduce the sauce by one-third. Remove the pan from the heat and stir in the remaining 1 tablespoon butter. Season to taste.

To serve: divide the apples among four warm appetizer plates. Top them with the liver slices and spoon the sauce over the top.

Serves 4.

David Robins'

Mesquite Grilled Cote De Boeuf
with Horseradish Potatoes and Green Peppercorn Sauce

*2 tablespoons fresh thyme leaves,
chopped*
*2 tablespoons coarsely cracked
black pepper*
*2 côtes de boeuf (a bone-on center-cut
ribeye; for this piece remove "cap"
and fat eye from whole rib strip and
cut into 22- to 24-ounce portions by
removing every other bone, resulting
in 2- to 3-inch-thick piece of meat
with a single bone attached)*
2 tablespoons extra-virgin olive oil
Salt

*Green Peppercorn Sauce
(recipe follows)*
Horseradish Potatoes (recipe follows)

For Green Peppercorn Sauce:
2 cups red wine
1 1/2 cups Port wine (ruby)
1 shallot, peeled and thinly sliced
4 sprigs fresh thyme
1 tablespoon whole black peppercorns
*1 1/2 cups unsalted chicken stock
(not canned)*
1/2 cup veal demiglace (veal stock

reduced to gelatinous state when cold)
*2 tablespoons green peppercorns,
canned in brine (remove from can and
soak 20 minutes in cold water; drain
and discard water)*
*2 tablespoons unsalted butter,
cut in 8 pieces*
Salt
Black pepper

For Horseradish Potatoes:
*1 pound small red potatoes (roughly 8
to 9, 2 inches in diameter), peeled*
Salt
1 cup sour cream
*1 to 3 tablespoons prepared
horseradish (the amount used depends
on your taste)*
2 tablespoons unsalted butter, melted
*Milk or cream, warm (for thinning
potatoes as necessary)*
Kosher salt
Ground white pepper

For côtes de boeuf: Mix the thyme and black pepper in a small bowl. Place on a plate and set aside.

Brush each côte de boeuf with the oil until coated well, then sprinkle generously with the thyme/pepper mixture to coat each side evenly.

Refrigerate 2 to 6 hours.

To cook, remove the côtes de boeuf from the refrigerator 30 minutes before cooking. Season well with salt on all sides. Prepare grill.

Cook over a hot fire for 6 to 8 minutes, rotating the meat well to brown. Pull the meat back away from hottest part of the fire and cook to desired doneness. When halfway cooked, remove the bone from the meat and grill separately. (This will allow the meat to cook more evenly and render any fat between the bone and the meat.) Rotate the meat frequently, being careful not to burn it. The cooking can take up to 30 minutes with a large piece of meat like the côte de boeuf, depending on the heat of the fire and thickness of the steak.

For green peppercorn sauce: Combine first five ingredients in small saucepot and bring to a boil over high heat. Reduce liquid by two-thirds until syrupy.

Strain the reduced wine mixture into a clean saucepan; add the chicken stock and reduce again by two-thirds.

Add the demiglace and reduce (low heat, low boil) 5 minutes until mixture is thickened.

Add the green peppercorns and reduce heat to very low. Gradually whisk the small pieces of butter into the sauce, adding the next piece when the first has completely melted. Season the sauce with salt and pepper to taste and serve.

For horseradish potatoes: Cook potatoes until soft in low-boiling salted water. Remove when completely soft but not breaking apart, drain well, and place into the bowl of an electric mixer fitted with a paddle attachment. Add sour cream, 1 tablespoon horseradish and melted butter and season lightly with salt and pepper.

Turn mixer on low and mix until just combined. Do not overmix! Taste the potatoes for seasoning and strength of horseradish. Add more horseradish if desired, remembering that a full portion can be very overwhelming if too spicy.

If mixture is very thick, thin it slightly with warm milk or cream. Check seasoning and serve.

This can be held warm surrounded by a water bath for up to two hours.

NOTE: The potatoes can also be mixed by hand if an electric mixer is unavailable. Remember not to mash, just mix until potatoes are all crushed.

To serve: Once meat is cooked to desired doneness, remove to a warm spot and allow to rest 4 to 5 minutes. Slice the steak thinly (¼ inch) and serve immediately with green peppercorn sauce, horseradish potatoes, and vegetable of your choice.

Serves 4.